Later Mesopotamia and Iran:
Tribes and Empires
1600–539 BC

Later Mesopotamia and Iran: Tribes and Empires 1600–539 BC

Proceedings of a Seminar in memory of
Vladimir G. Lukonin

Funded by a gift from
Raymond and Beverly Sackler

Edited by John Curtis

Published for the Trustees of the British Museum by
British Museum Press

© 1995 The Trustees of the British Museum

Published by British Museum Press
A division of British Museum Publications
46 Bloomsbury Street, London WC1B 3QQ

A catalogue record for this book is available
from the British Library

ISBN 07141 1138 4

Designed by Andrew Shoolbred
Printed and bound in Great Britain by
The Bath Press, Avon

Front jacket: Three female figures of the Middle
Elamite period, *c*.1500–1000 BC, from a collection of
about 200 examples found by W.K. Loftus at Susa.
Back jacket: *Kudurru* (boundary stone) of
Marduk-nadin-ahhe, king of Babylon 1099–1082 BC.

Contents

Acknowledgements

In the preparation of this volume help has been received from a number of quarters. Bernadette Heaney put the text on disk, and Barbara Winter and John Heffron of the British Museum Photographic Service kindly undertook – at short notice – to do some of the photographic work. Several of the maps were prepared by Ann Searight. The volume was prepared for publication with her customary skill by Carolyn Jones of the British Museum Press, and best thanks are due to her for her patience and efficiency. Last, but certainly not least, thanks are again due to Raymond and Beverly Sackler who not only supported the lecture series but also sponsored this publication, thus ensuring that the results of the seminar would be published and made available to a wider audience.

List of Illustrations

Black and white plates

Preface

by John Curtis

In this volume are published the proceedings of a seminar held in the British Museum on 14 July 1993 on the subject of relations between Mesopotamia and Iran in the period between the collapse of the First Dynasty of Babylon, soon after 1600 BC, and 539 BC when Cyrus the Great captured Babylon and the Near East fell under the control of the Achaemenid Persians. Four eminent specialists were invited to participate in the seminar and speak about different aspects of this complex but highly intriguing subject. Agnès Spycket, a curator in the Département des Antiquités Orientales at the Musée du Louvre, reviewed Kassite sculpture in Mesopotamia and compared it with contemporary Middle Elamite sculpture in Iran. Peter Calmeyer of the Deutsches Archäologisches Institut in Berlin, who was formerly based in Tehran, looked at Babylonian art in the time of the Kassite and Second Dynasty of Isin kings and demonstrated connections with the art of Iran. Contact between the two areas was particularly close in the Kassite period when Kassite civilisation extended along the River Diyala into the Zagros Mountains of Western Iran. Louis Vanden Berghe of the University of Gent concentrated on the results of his excavations in the Pusht-i Kuh, the western part of Luristan, where he excavated a large number of cemetery sites between 1965 and 1979. He reviewed the wealth of material of Iron III date and pointed to comparisons with Assyria. Although the contacts were quite marked in some cases, it was clear that on the whole Luristan was a self-contained area that retained a strongly independent and distinctive art style of its own. Sadly, Professor Vanden Berghe died just two months after the seminar.[1] At the event itself failing eyesight had prevented him from delivering his paper in person, which task fell to his young collaborator Alexander Tourovets. Vanden Berghe was able, however, to introduce the paper, and his participation in the seminar was greatly appreciated by all his friends and colleagues in Britain. His passing leaves a gap in the ranks of

1 The speakers at the Lukonin Memorial Seminar in July 1993. From left: Professor Peter Calmeyer; Madame Agnès Spycket; Dr Michael Roaf; Professor Louis Vanden Berghe.

Iranian archaeologists which it will be difficult to fill. He was one of the most distinguished archaeologists of his generation but he was much more than simply a dirt archaeologist and his contributions to Iranian studies have been immense. They have included important works of synthesis and reference that are fundamental for any study of Ancient Iran. To conclude the proceedings, Michael Roaf outlined the historical contacts between Media and Mesopotamia, specifically Assyria, and contrasted the architectural styles in the two regions. For the purpose of this exercise attention was focused on Tepe Nush-i Jan, until now the best-known Median site. Dr Roaf is particularly well qualified to talk about Nush-i Jan because he worked with David Stronach in all five campaigns at this site between 1967 and 1977, in the latter stages as Assistant Director.

The seminar held in 1993, the proceedings of which are published here, was in fact the fifth annual lecture or seminar held at the British Museum in memory of the distinguished Russian scholar Vladimir G. Lukonin (1932–84) who was head of the Oriental Department at the State Hermitage in St. Petersburg. This series has been made possible through the great generosity of Raymond and Beverly Sackler who have provided the necessary endowment. Originally, the idea of a lecture series was mooted at a reception to mark the inauguration of the Lukonin Memorial Fund, now renamed the Ancient Persia Fund in memory of Vladimir G. Lukonin. This Fund, set up on the initiative of the Hon. Mrs Mary Anna Marten, was established to promote the study of

2 Lord Windlesham and Raymond and Beverly Sackler at the opening of the Later Mesopotamia Gallery in July 1993.

3 HRH Princess Margaret with Raymond and Beverly Sackler at the opening of the Later Mesopotamia Gallery in July 1993.

4 Professor Ezat O. Negahban.

Ancient Iran. At present it gives annual grants for travel and study to scholars and students working on Ancient Iran and related subjects. The lecture series began in 1989 with Academician Boris Piotrovskii, the erstwhile Director of the State Hermitage, talking about 'Ancient Iran and the Caucasus'. Then in 1990 Professor Robert H. Dyson, Jr, then Director of the University Museum of the University of Pennsylvania, spoke about 'Hasanlu and Iron Age Iron'. In 1991 was the first Lukonin seminar, when four distinguished scholars were invited to present lectures on the subject of relations between Iran and Mesopotamia in the early historical periods. The participants were Monsieur Pierre Amiet, Dr Roger Moorey, Professor Hans Nissen and Professor Edith Porada, now sadly deceased.[2] The proceedings of this seminar were published by British Museum Press in 1993 under the title *Early Mesopotamia and Iran: Contact and Conflict 3500– 1600 BC*. The present book is intended as a sequel to that volume.

The 1992 lecture was given by Professor Ezat O. Negahban, formerly of the University of Tehran and since 1980 Visiting Guest Curator of Iranian Archaeology in the Near Eastern Section of the University Museum of the University of Pennsylvania. He has the distinction of being the most famous archaeologist that Iran has yet produced and particularly through his excavations at Marlik in Gilan and at Haft Tepe in Khuzistan, and his subsequent publications, he has made fundamental contributions to our knowledge of Ancient Iran. It was about one of these sites, Marlik, that he spoke on 16 July. The lecture was entitled 'The Treasures of Marlik and Late Bronze Age Iran'. Professor Negahban described how the site was found in 1961 in the course of making an archaeological map of Iran. After a single test trench had produced many valuable objects, excavations continued for fourteen months. Fifty-three tombs were found with a wealth of material mainly dating from the late second millennium BC. From these tombs about 25,000 items were recovered, the most spectacular of them being gold and silver vessels and hollow pottery figurines of men and animals in red or grey burnished pottery. Although the mound of Marlik was inhabited by venomous snakes – which is perhaps reflected in the name of the site, the Persian word *mar* meaning snake – an even greater danger for the archaeologists was posed by clandestine diggers. Once news spread of the valuable antiquities being discovered, the archaeologists were much troubled by antiquities dealers who were in league with corrupt government officials. They stopped at nothing to get their hands on the treasures, and to prevent illegal excavations the archaeologists had to stay up at night on watch. In spite of this they were powerless to prevent nocturnal raids, and Negahban showed a dramatic picture of how his own tent was slashed open in an attempt to steal the antiquities. Because of these problems the excavation turned into a sort of military camp, but nothing daunted Professor Negahban continued until there was a change of government in 1962. It because clear from Professor Negahban's lecture that in view of the very difficult circumstances the success of the excavations was even more remarkable.

The seminar in 1993 was timed to coincide with the opening of the new Raymond and Beverly Sackler galleries of Later Mesopotamia (Room 55) and Anatolia (Rooms 53–54) which had taken place the previous day, on 13 July. The completion of these new rooms extends the suite of galleries refurbished and reorganised thanks to the generosity of the Sacklers. An exhibition devoted to Early Mesopotamia was opened in 1991. On both occasions the galleries were graciously opened by HRH Princess Margaret. With these new exhibitions the opportunity has been taken completely to reorganise the old displays and to bring out much material that was previously in store. Although a few people may regret the demise of old displays such as the Room of Writing the aim now is not to concentrate on thematic presentations but to give a rounded picture of civilisations such as Mesopotamia. This can best be done by including in an exhibition all the different elements which together make up the material culture, and these include seals and cuneiform tablets. As well as upgrading the exhibitions new display cases have been installed and some necessary building works undertaken.

Notes

1 See Curtis 1994.
2 See Collon 1994.

Introduction

by John Curtis

The period from the middle of the second millennium BC until the Persian conquest in 539 BC was a momentous time in the development of the Ancient Near East, not least for relations between Mesopotamia and Iran. During this thousand-year timespan new peoples entered Iran, and the Assyrian and Babylonian empires successively controlled large parts of the Near East.

In 1595 BC, Babylon was sacked by the Hittite king Mursilis, bringing to an end the rule of the so-called First Dynasty of Babylon, whose most illustrious member had been Hammurabi. There followed an obscure period of some 150 years. In northern Mesopotamia the Hurrian kingdom of Mitanni was dominant, while in the south Kassite kings ruled Babylon at least from the late fifteenth century onwards. The Kassites were immigrants to Babylonia, but where exactly they came from is not known. What is certain, however, is that their sphere of influence extended into western Iran, mainly along the line of the River Diyala. It is probably for this reason that bronze daggers inscribed with the names of Babylonian kings and officials, dating from the Late Kassite period and the Second Dynasty of Isin, have allegedly been found inside modern Iran. Unfortunately, none of these daggers comes from a controlled excavation. There are two examples in the British Museum (Pl. 1; Moorey 1974: pl. IIA-B). One is inscribed with the name of Marduk-nadin-ahhe, king of Babylon (1099–1082 BC) and the other is recorded as being the property of Shamash-killanni, the eunuch of a king. Also supposed to have been found in Iran, but again largely unprovenanced, are embossed bronze beakers in Babylonian style often showing figures seated on thrones. An example in the British Museum (Col. Pl. I; Moorey 1974: pl. XVII) has a design of goats on either side of a stylised tree. Another has an enthroned figure, accompanied by two attendants sitting in front of a cross-legged table (BM 134735; Calmeyer 1973: pl. 4, no. A18). Peter Calmeyer, who has written an important monograph about these

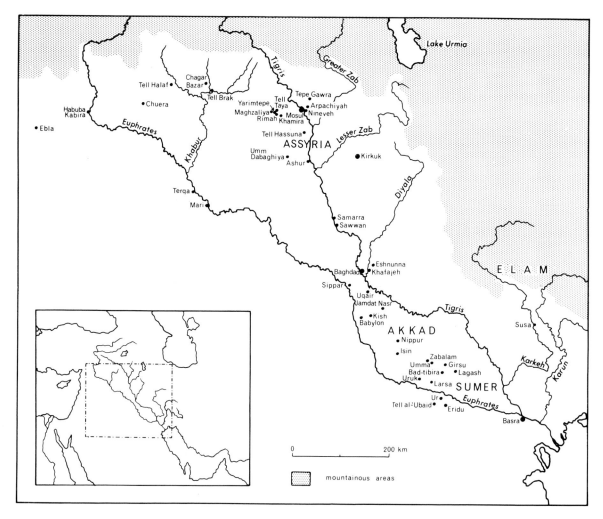

5 Map of Mesopotamia.

beakers (Calmeyer 1973), dates them to the tenth century BC. He returns to this subject in his chapter below. In northern Mesopotamia the decline of Mitannian power left the way open for the dramatic expansion of the state that in the first millennium BC was to dominate the whole of the Ancient Near East, namely Assyria. This growth in the so-called Middle Assyrian period was largely achieved under three outstanding military leaders, Adad-Nirari I (1307–1275 BC), Shalmaneser I (1274–45 BC) and Tukulti-Ninurta I (1244–08 BC).

In Iran, equally significant events were taking place in this period. In the lowland area in the south-west, Elamite civilisation enjoyed a splendid period, reaching its peak under Untash-Napirisha (c.1340–1300 BC) who undertook much building work at Susa and founded a new city 40 km to the south-east, now known as Choga Zanbil. In the twelfth century, Elamite kings such as Shutruk-Nahhunte and his son Kutir-Nahhunte mounted raids deep into Mesopotamia and

16

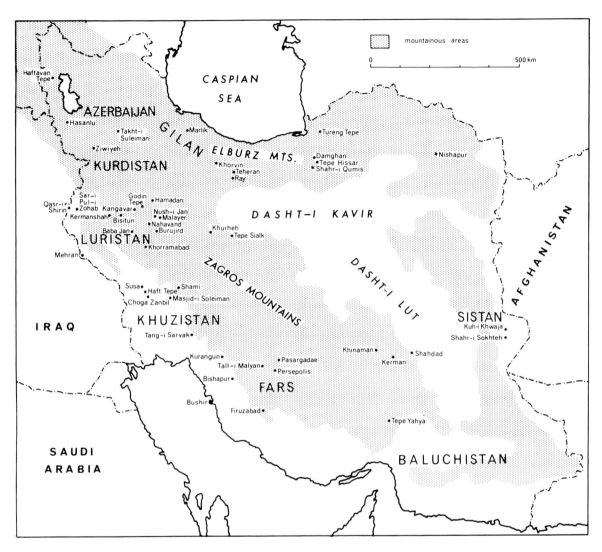

6 Map of Iran.

carried off treasures and works of art including a stela engraved with the laws of Hammurabi. But the tables were turned by Nebuchadnezzar I (1125–1104 BC) of the Second Dynasty of Isin who looted Susa. The splendour of the Middle Elamite period is attested particularly at Susa, where many important objects of this date have been found. They come mainly from the French excavations, and Agnès Spycket describes below some of the more interesting examples of statuary. But before the French started work, W.K. Loftus excavated at Susa in the years 1850–52 (Curtis 1993). This has resulted in a small collection of Susa material being now at the British Museum, including about forty terracotta figurines of the same distinctive type showing women with enormously fat hips, naked except for a few pieces of jewellery and some sort of headdress.

Their hands are cupped under their breasts (dust-jacket). More examples were found by the later French excavators (e.g. pls 15, 17–18).

To the north of Elam, on the Iranian Plateau and in the eastern foothills of the Zagros Mountains, this period witnessed the arrival of tribes speaking Indo-Iranian languages. The introduction of new pottery forms, particularly vessels in a distinctive sort of grey ware, dates to this time and the dead were now buried in cemeteries. These innovations are often connected with the Indo-European migrations, but the association remains hypothetical. One of the sites at which a form of this grey ware pottery has been found is Marlik in Gilan, in the lush area between the Elburz Mountains and the Caspian Sea. Here, Professor Negahban opened more than fifty tombs in 1961–2, as he dramatically described in the 1992 Lukonin lecture. The rich finds from these graves included large pottery figurines, both of humans and animals. Hump-backed bulls were particularly popular. Gold and silver beakers with concave sides are particularly diagnostic of Marlik: they have cable-pattern borders at top and bottom, and geometric rosettes on the base. The embossed designs on the sides often show winged bulls and other mythical beasts. There are also many beakers of this kind from unofficial excavations, presumably at Marlik or in the vicinity. A complete silver example in the British Museum (Col. Pl. II; Curtis 1989a: pl. 19) shows horses in the upper register and winged lions attacking ibexes in the lower register. These graves at Marlik, dating mainly between c.1400 and 1000 BC, provide evidence of a rich and flourishing culture that is essentially local in inspiration. Direct contact with Assyria may not have existed, but there are certainly some interesting parallels in the material culture. In Middle Assyrian seals of the thirteenth-twelfth century BC there is, as Edith Porada remarked, 'a prominence of monstrous or demonic combinations of creatures' (Porada 1992: 184).[1] It cannot be coincidence that such monsters are a familiar feature on the Marlik beakers. We may also refer to mosaic glass, which was popular both at Middle Assyrian sites such as Tell al-Rimah (Col. Pl. III; Barag 1985: pl. A4) and at Marlik (Col. Pl. IV; Negahban 1964: pl. XVII), although of course the form was different.

A key site for our knowledge of the late second and early first millennium BC in Western Iran is Hasanlu, a large mound in the Solduz Valley to the south-west of Lake Urmia (Col. Pl. V). The Early Iron Age (or Iron I period, c.1450–1250 BC) is represented at Hasanlu by the remains of buildings known as Hasanlu period V. Also dating from this time are large quantities of burnished pottery, chiefly in grey but also in red. This type of pottery is quite different from that of the preceding Bronze Age. The excavator himself has summed up the situation in this way: 'Hasanlu period V represents not only a sudden change in pottery form and manufacturing technology, but also new burial rituals, new types of clothing and ornaments, and new architectural practices and building plans' (Dyson and Voigt 1989: 108). In the next period (Iron II) there was a series of columned buildings arranged around courtyards which were twice destroyed by fire. The first marked the end of the Hasanlu IVC phase in c.1100 BC and the second and more disastrous conflagration destroyed the Hasanlu IVB settlement. In the ruins were found both the bodies of humans who had been overcome while trying to escape from the fire and a rich assortment of objects, providing us with a fascinating picture of the material culture of this period. The destruction debris of Hasanlu IVB is said to have been full of 'Assyrian related material' (Dyson and Muscarella 1989: 3), which was found alongside objects showing both local and north Syrian influence. For example, six of the twenty-one cylinder seals are regarded by Michelle Marcus as actual Assyrian products (Marcus 1990: 135) and there are Assyrian-style ivories (Muscarella 1980: nos 280–293). A glazed wall-tile (Dyson and Voigt 1989: fig. 10a) is comparable with ninth-century examples found at Nimrud and Balawat in Assyria. When was this settlement at Hasanlu destroyed? It used to be universally accepted that the site was burned by the Urartians in about 800 BC. However, in a provocative article published a few years ago in *Iran*, Inna Medvedskaya (1988) has argued that the mono-ring horsebits with three-hole cheekpieces and trapezoidal noseguards for horses found in the destruction level cannot be earlier than the mid-eighth century BC. Also, she argues that the ivories depicting chariots and riders show details of harness and horsemanship that are incompatible with a ninth century date. She therefore concludes that Hasanlu was destroyed by King Sargon of Assyria during his so-called eighth campaign in 714 BC. Dyson and Muscarella have refuted these arguments and have replied with a barrage of radiocarbon dates that are not in themselves conclusive (1989).[2] Nevertheless, a cogent argument is the fact that inscriptions of the Urartian kings Ishpuini and Menua at Kel-i Shin, Qalatgah and elsewhere show that the area around Hasanlu came under Urartian control from the late ninth century onwards. If the Hasanlu IVB settlement had continued until 714, therefore, there ought to be some evidence of Urartian influence. On the contrary, amongst the objects from the debris of Hasanlu IVB practically no Urartian influence is visible, and there is no identifiable Urartian pottery (Dyson and Muscarella 1989: 19–20, 22). Urartian influence only becomes obvious later. After the destruction of Level IVB there was a squatter occupation (IVA), followed, after a period of abandonment, by the construction of a massive fortification wall around the top of the mound (IIIB). Associated with this occupation level were 'sherds of polished red ware of Urartian type' (Dyson and Muscarella 1989: 2–3). Another telling fact, noted by Dr Tamas Dezso of Budapest in a forthcoming monograph on Ancient Near Eastern helmets, is that in the destruction debris of Hasanlu IVB, and apparently in use at that time, are two types of bronze helmet, crested and pointed. The only time when these two types of helmet could have been in use together was around 800 BC.

Final judgement may have to be reserved until the full publication of the 7000 artefacts said to have been recovered from the debris of Hasanlu IVB (Dyson and Muscarella 1989: 1, 19–20), but as matters stand at present it does seem more likely that Hasanlu IVB was destroyed at the beginning of the eighth century rather than towards the end of the eighth century, although the round date of 800 BC may have to be revised and perhaps slightly lowered in due course.

In either scenario, the alleged absence of Assyrian or Assyrianising material in Hasanlu IIIB (Dyson and Muscarella 1989: 3), that in the excavator's view lasted c 750–600 BC, is odd. It is certainly true that the ninth century Assyrian kings Ashurnasirpal II and Shalmaneser III campaigned actively in Iran, which perhaps partly accounts for the considerable Assyrian influence noticed in Hasanlu IVB, but many of their successors also campaigned in the Zagros Mountains and penetrated Western Iran to some degree. The Assyrians may even have approached Tehran if the Mount Bikni of the texts is correctly identified as Mount Demavend, the tallest peak in the Elburz range; this identification is suggested because of the association of Mount Bikni with the salt desert, presumably the Dasht-i Kavir.[3] Sometimes, the Assyrian kings left behind memorials recording their campaigns in Iran. For example, stelae carved on rockfaces are known at Shikaft-i Gulgul in Luristan, probably from the reign of Ashurbanipal (Reade 1977), and at Tang-i Var (Uramanat) in Kurdistan, probably dating from the reigns of Tiglath-pileser III or Sargon (Col. Pl. VI; Sarfaraz 1969). The latter example is not yet published. There is also a freestanding stela of Sargon II found at Najafehabad, 15 km northeast of Kangavar (Levine 1972: 25–58).[4] With all this Assyrian activity in Iran, then, the lack of Assyrian influence in Hasanlu IIIB is surprising. But it is not only intermittent Assyrian military presence in Iran that might have been expected to result in Assyrian influence. From their homeland on the river Tigris in Northern Iraq, with capital cites successively at Ashur, Nimrud, Khorsabad and Nineveh, the Assyrians built up an empire that at its greatest extent stretched to the Mediterranean coast and even into Egypt. Some parts of Western Iran were also more or less under Assyrian control. In effect Assyria dominated the Ancient Near East, and its prosperity is dramatically illustrated by the contents of four tombs discovered at Nimrud between spring 1988 and November 1990. These tombs apparently belong to a number of Assyrian queens and are in a wing of the North-West Palace that may have been a harem. They contained an astonishing array of jewellery and vessels in precious metal. It is estimated there were 14 kg of gold objects in the second tomb and 23 kg in the third. In view of the extraordinary wealth and power of Assyria, it is hardly surprising that the material culture of the whole area was influenced by Assyrian art and traditions. In this respect, Iran was no exception. The Assyrian impact on Luristan is discussed below by Louis Vanden Berghe. We have already remarked on the presence of Assyrian and Assyrianising material in Hasanlu IV (Iron II period), and it is likely that this phenomenon became more marked in the following Iron III period (but not at Hasanlu). In fact, there is a good deal of evidence for Assyrian influence at this time. Some of it is well documented, and comes from properly excavated sites such as Tepe Nush-i Jan, as we shall see below, but unfortunately much of the evidence revolves around unprovenanced material and illegal excavations.

For example, in 1985 Mr Ismail Yaghmayi of the Muzeh Melli (Iran Bastan Museum) in Tehran undertook rescue excavations at a site near the village of Ghallat, situated between Bukan and Takht-e Suleiman and about 30 km north of Ziwiyeh. He found traces of a building decorated with polychrome glazed tiles and an Aramaic inscription which has not yet been published (Curtis, V.S., 1988; Mousavi 1994: 7–8). Unfortunately, the site had already been extensively plundered, and many tiles that have appeared on the art market are believed to come from Ghallat. Altogether there are well over 100 tiles in circulation. There is an extraordinary range of designs and motifs on these tiles, including human-headed winged bulls, winged sphinxes, ibexes, lions, birds of prey, winged genies, and monstrous hybrid animals as well as floral and geometric motifs. The strong Assyrian influence is unmistakable, and it is likely the tiles date from around the reign of Sargon (721–705 BC).

This Assyrian influence even extended as far as Elam, which in view of Assyria's relations with Elam is surprising. After the splendours of the Middle Elamite period Susa went through a period of decline. This was partly because the Elamites were blocked in by the Medes to the north and north-east and by the Assyrians to the north-west who controlled the Diyala Valley. But late in the eighth century there was a renaissance and for nearly a century Elam challenged the authority of Assyria (Harper *et al.* 1992: 197). Elamite resistance usually took the form of supporting the Babylonians who in one way or another were forever trying to throw off the Assyrian yoke. Matters came to a head in the reign of Ashurbanipal, when in a pitched battle at Tell Tuba on the River Ulai in 653 BC the Elamites were defeated and their king Teumman killed (Grayson 1991: 147–8). These events are graphically depicted in the stone reliefs decorating the Assyrian palaces at Nineveh (Reade 1976). On this occasion the Assyrians apparently withdrew without devastating the country, but a few years later, after the Elamites had supported yet another Babylonian rebellion, Ashurbanipal had no choice but to turn the full strength of the Assyrian military machine against Elam. This culminated in the sack and destruction of Susa in 646 BC, after which Elam ceased to exist as a major political power (Grayson 1991: 149–54).

Testifying to Assyrian contacts with this area are the contents of an important tomb discovered by chance in 1982 at Arjan near Behbehan in Khuzistan, about 250 km south-east of Susa (Alizadeh 1985). The body was buried in a bronze coffin with straight sides, rounded at one end and squared-off at the other, and with a pair of handles at either end (Fig. 7a). I have attempted elsewhere to show that this type of bronze coffin is Assyrian and that they should be dated to the late eighth century BC (Curtis 1983). Three more of these coffins have recently been discovered in the third of the royal tombs at Nimrud. Associated with the burial was a gold bracelet with the terminals decorated with winged lions (Fig. 7b). This is obviously later than the coffin, perhaps even as late as the Achaemenid period. A bronze stand, *c.* 75 cm high (Fig. 7c), has at the bottom Atlas figures in Mesopotamian style of a type associated on the Assyrian reliefs with furniture in the reigns of Sargon (721–705 BC) and Sennacherib (704–681 BC) (Baker 1966: figs. 295, 299–301). However, the bull protomes at the base and the lions with twisted heads above them suggest a rather later date. There were also in the tomb gold clothing ornaments, a dagger with an iron blade, a silver rod, a silver jar and a number of bronze vessels. Amongst the latter was a large bronze bowl, 43.5 cm in diameter, with intricate incised decoration in five registers surrounding a central rosette (Sarraf 1990; Majidzadeh 1992). These show scenes of banqueting, presentation, hunting and date-harvesting. The Assyrian influence here is obvious, although the bowl was not necessarily made in Assyria. Iconographic features such as the furniture and the chariots indicate that the bowl cannot be earlier than the reign of Sargon and probably dates from around the time of Ashurbanipal (668–627 BC). Both the bowl and the gold bracelet bear an Elamite inscription recording the name of Kidin-Hutran, son of Kurlush. F. Vallat has argued that this Kidin-Hutran must have reigned in the period between 646 BC and 539 or 520 BC (Vallat 1984).

What, then, can be concluded about the date of this tomb? In his publication, Alizadeh opted for a date in the first half of the eighth century BC, a date which cannot be reconciled with the evidence of the inscriptions as interpreted by Vallat. In a review of Alizadeh's article, Boehmer (1989: 142–3) has proposed a date for the tomb at the end of the seventh century or in the first half of the sixth century BC. Of course, there is no certainty that we are dealing with a single burial:

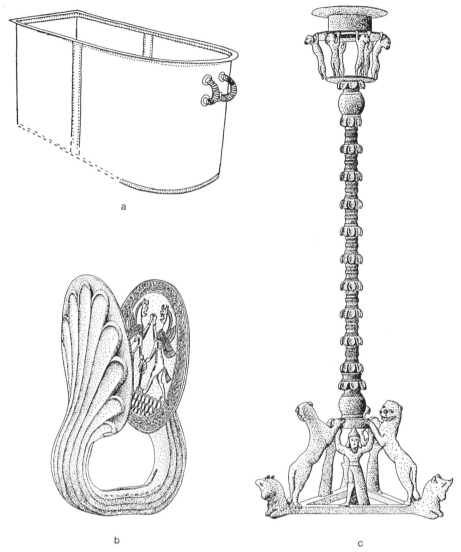

7 A bronze coffin, gold bracelet and bronze stand from a tomb at Arjan near Behbehan, Iran.

the coffin may have been re-used, which would account for the apparently different dates of the material. However, if we do have a single, undisturbed burial, then a date of around 600 BC or later, as proposed by Boehmer, does seem most likely, although in this case the coffin would have been more than a century old when it was used.

Further north, in Media, the situation was different. Whereas in Elam the inhabitants had their own written language (Elamite) and to a certain extent had a culture than was distinctively their own, this was not really the case with the Medes. They were an Indo-Iranian tribe speaking an Iranian language, but we do not know if they were literate. They first appear in the historical record in the ninth century BC when they are mentioned in contemporary Assyrian texts.

Thereafter they were in frequent conflict with the Assyrians, but relations were not always hostile. In the reign of Esarhaddon the Medes were among the subject peoples who promised to recognise the succession to the throne of Assyria, and their oaths to this effect are preserved in the so-called 'vassal treaties' (Grayson 1991: 129). By the seventh century BC they were established in an area bounded by Hamadan (ancient Ecbatana, their capital), Malayer and Kangavar, that is known as 'the Median triangle'. Only two Iron III sites have as yet been excavated in the Median heartland, of which one is Godin Tepe, where there were interesting buildings but no significant small finds from the Level II settlement. The other is Tepe Nush-i Jan, excavated by David Stronach between 1967 and 1977. What does it tell us about the lifestyle of the Medes? Many of the objects found here such as tools, weapons, beads and fibulae are of the type that can be found at many Near Eastern sites at this time and are not diagnostic of a particular culture. But some other finds demonstrate clear Assyrian connections. There is, for example, a bronze pendant of the Meso-potamian demon, Pazuzu (Curtis 1984: no. 296). Then, there is a black stone stamp seal that shows a cow and calf with a star and four or five dots above (Fig. 8a; ibid.: no. 233). This is a popular scene in Assyria, and is closely paralleled on seals from Nimrud (eg. Mallowan 1966: I, figs. 134/5, 241). A cylinder seal impression shows an archer shooting at a snake (Fig. 8b; Curtis 1984: no. 236). It is related to a group of Late Assyrian faience seals with similar scenes, examples of which are known from Ashur, Khorsabad and Tell Halaf. A second stamp seal, of faience and showing a boat with upturned prow and stern, a stylised tree and an offering-stand (Fig. 8c; ibid.: no. 234), is related to a group of Syro-Phoenician seals thought to show Isis in the solar barque. Although not Assyrian, this seal is certainly of a type that might have been current in the Assyrian Empire. The interesting question here is whether these items are direct imports from Assyria, or whether they are local copies of Assyrian originals. If the latter, it would demonstrate that Median material culture, at least in some aspects, was heavily dependent on Assyria.[5] However, this does not apply to the pottery which was quite distinctive (Col. Pl. VII). Median architecture is considered below by Michael Roaf.

By 612 BC the Medes were a power to be reckoned with. In that year, in conjunction with the Babylonians, they overran Assyria and sacked the major Assyrian cities such as Nimrud and Nineveh. The former Assyrian empire was carved up between the two new powers. In the east, the

a

b

c

8 Drawings of seals from Tepe Nush-i Jan, Iran.

approximate boundary between them probably ran up the River Tigris and along the Lesser Zab so that, at least from about 590 BC, the Assyrian heartland was under Median control (Curtis 1989b: 52–4).[6] However, the history of this period is still obscure, and even if the Medes were in charge of northern Iraq it is unlikely that they exercised any administrative control over the area. The western part of the Assyrian empire, mainly Syria and Phoenicia, fell to the Babylonians, but not before an Egyptian army had been defeated near Hama in 605 BC. There were also other difficulties. Nebuchadnezzar (604–562 BC), certainly the best-known Babylonian king, twice laid siege to Jerusalem and carried off many of its inhabitants to captivity in Babylon. It was also Nebuchadnezzar who was largely responsible for the building programme at Babylon, which resulted in the city becoming an object of wonder and envy in the ancient world. Its legendary walls, however, on the top of which, according to Herodotus, a chariot could turn around, were not enough to keep out Cyrus the Great. He entered Babylon in 539 BC, and shortly thereafter the whole of the Near East fell under Persian rule.

Notes

1 Monstrous forms were also popular amongst the Hurrians. See Porada 1979 and Porada 1992: 184.
2 Medvedskaya has replied in an article in *Iranica Antiqua*, restating her original position (Medvedskaya 1991). In a review of Dyson and Voigt 1989, Moorey writes that 'the debate remains delicately balanced' (Moorey 1993: 320).
3 Grayson (1991: 80, 129) prefers the identification of Bikni with Mt. Alvand near Hamadan.
4 A freestanding stela of Tiglath-pileser III (Levine 1972: 11–24) is alleged to have been found in western Iran, possibly Luristan, but the exact

provenance is unfortunately unknown. Further bibliographical references to these Assyrian monuments will be found in Börker-Klähn 1982, under nos 171, 173, 223 and 248.
5 It is important to stress that these items are examples of Median material culture and not of Median art. It cannot be disputed that the *inspiration* came from Assyria. For a cautionary essay on the subject of 'Median art', see Muscarella 1987.
6 See also Zawadzki 1988: 127, n. 22, 150.

Kassite and Middle Elamite Sculpture

by Agnès Spycket
MUSÉE DU LOUVRE, PARIS

It is a hazardous undertaking to deal with Kassite and Middle Elamite sculpture, because in fact this period of about four centuries, between the sixteenth and the twelfth century BC, is, as far as we know, rather poor in sculptural material. The reason does not stem primarily from the accident of archaeological discovery, but it is more probably due to the insecurity of these times, which were not really suitable for the development of a royal or an official art. This is particularly true for the Kassite dynasty which has left very little artistic evidence. On the other hand in Elam, the reign of king Untash-Napirisha heralded a flourishing development during the fourteenth century, but we can only guess at its one-time richness from the small number of existing examples.

We will consider here three aspects of sculpture: royal, popular and funerary.

Royal Sculpture

We have remains of sculpture from the reigns of only two Kassite kings. The first of these, Karaindash, dedicated a small temple to Inanna in Warka in the fifteenth century BC (Amiet 1977: fig. 86). The tradition of decorating baked brick façades with slits and niches goes back to earlier times, but a new development here was to set in the niches engaged statues in moulded terracotta. There are gods alternating with goddesses holding the flowing vase, a theme well known in Mesopotamia. This technique of moulded bricks was very popular in Elam, not only in Achaemenid times, but already in the Middle Elamite period when panels of such bricks decorated the exterior of a temple of Inshushinak in Susa, built in the twelfth century BC by the kings Kutir-Nahhunte and Shilhak-Inshushinak (Amiet 1988: 104–5). Dating from this last king is moulded brick decoration with green and yellow glaze (Pl. 2), the elements of which were put together again by Pierre Amiet in the Musée du Louvre in 1976 (Amiet 1976b).

Although we have very little from the reign of Karaindash, we do not know much more about his second successor, Kurigalzu I, at the beginning of the fourteenth century. He probably founded the capital Dur-Kurigalzu (known today as 'Aqar Quf). We are not sure whether the poor remains of a colossal seated statue in diorite, found in a temple at 'Aqar Quf (Baqir 1944: 11, fig. 20; Kramer *et al.* 1948), belong to him or to Kurigalzu II who reigned in the second half of the fourteenth century. We can only remark that the Kassite sovereigns adopted the tradition and taste of their predecessors for diorite as the royal stone. The shoulder of a limestone statuette found in Susa is inscribed with the name of Kurigalzu who prides himself on 'having laid low Susa and Elam and overthrown Marhashi' on the Iranian plateau (Scheil 1939: 11–12, no. 9). Other texts relate the conquest of Susa and Elam at that time, but it is not clear which Kurigalzu is involved (Carter and Stolper 1984: 35). There was also a statue of king Melishipak, well known from a *kudurru* (boundary stone) of the twelfth century, but it was plundered by Shutruk-Nahhunte with other statues and has disappeared (Labat 1975: 486).

A terracotta male head (Pl. 3, ht. 4.3 cm) found in the palace at Dur-Kurigalzu deserves to be considered as a royal sculpture, in spite of its small size (Frankfort 1954: pl. 70B). The face, painted ochre, is delicate; the drawn out and slightly oblique eyes are outlined in black with a white cornea; the nose is aquiline; the red lips are carefully delineated; and the cheek-bones are framed by a short curly beard, painted in black. The hair is parted in the middle and a side plait, ending in a curl, falls onto the neck. In spite of the fact that the back of the head and most of the hair are missing, this head has noble qualities and we think that it might portray a Syrian dignitary.

A mutilated clay figurine found at Isin (Col. Pl. VIII) in 1988 in the temenos of the Gula Temple (Spycket 1992b: 57, no. 1B 1859, pls 45, 47) is similarly of painted terracotta. The man stands out from a background in high relief. The head and the lower part of the legs are missing. The upper body is naked, clearly showing the ribs. A long plain skirt is held at the waist by a belt in high relief. The right arm hangs down by the body, while the left is held across the chest. As on the 'Aqar Quf head the flesh is painted red. The skirt is now brown, but judging from traces of white, it must once have been of this colour. The belt is dark brown. In spite of its poor state of preservation, the similarity of the pose with that of a man painted on the wall of the palace of Kurigalzu at 'Aqar Quf (Col. Pl. IX; Parrot 1961: fig. 335) is quite striking.

Scarcely worth mentioning is a small female head, ht. 7 cm, in white limestone, of very bad quality (Pl. 4) that is broken off at the shoulders. It was found at Ur in a Kurigalzu level (Woolley 1965: pl. 28, U17865). The hairdo, originally fixed by a dowel to the top of the head, has disappeared. The ears were drilled for earrings. This coarse face with its inlaid eyes hardly deserved to be handed down to posterity, but this object must have been valued in antiquity because it was broken then and mended with bitumen, the glue of the Ancient Near East. More refined, but alas! also very damaged, is a female head from Ashur, ht. 11 cm, in alabaster (Pl. 5). It was discovered in a temple built by Tukulti-Ninurta I, and so probably dates from the thirteenth century BC. The face is very abraded and the nose and mouth destroyed. The eyes were inlaid. The hair falls onto the shoulders and there is a flat cap on top of the head.

Compared with these stray pieces, the lifesize statue or rather the torso of a naked woman, inscribed by the Assyrian king Ashur-bel-kala (Spycket 1981: 303–5, pls 197a-b), stands out as a real masterpiece (Pl. 6). In spite of the mutilation which has deprived it of its head, arms and feet, this beautiful stone sculpture remains one of the best pieces in the Department of Western Asiatic Antiquities at the British Museum and it has attracted much comment. Discovered at Nineveh by Rassam in 1853, it is well proportioned and the soberness of the detail is amazing. Neither the breasts nor the buttocks are pronounced and the conjoined legs taper only slightly towards the bottom. While, as we shall see below, the representation of naked women is widespread on the small clay figurines of popular tradition, the occurrence of such a large statue is unique up to the present time. Because of its size and its nakedness it is generally supposed to be a goddess, and on account of the lack of detail, we have suggested that this statue was made to be dressed and presented to the faithful at ceremonies, as described in Babylonian texts gathered in 1949 by Leo Oppenheim. His article is illustrated by deities adorned with magnificent clothes on reliefs or *kudurru*, of later date than the statue but still significant (Fig. 9; Oppenheim 1949). These practices are described in the Old Testament (eg. Jeremiah X.1–16) and they are again con-demned in a Greek text of the second century BC that forms part of the Apocryphal Book of Baruch. This Epistle of Jeremiah purports to have been written by the prophet to the Exiles in Babylon. We read: 'But now shall ye see in Babylon gods of silver, and of gold, and of wood, borne upon shoulders . . . and they deck them as men with garments . . . Yet cannot these gods save themselves from rust and moths, though they be covered with purple raiment' (Revised English Bible, Baruch VI.4, 11–12). Of course, we cannot know for certain whether the statue was exhibited dressed or not, and there are also doubts about its origin and its date. What is indisputable is that it was discovered at the capital of Assyria and the seven-line inscription engraved on the back, above the waist, dates from the eleventh century BC, as it mentions the palace of king Ashur-bel-kala, son of Tiglath-pileser I. However, although there is a lack of comparative material, the statue recalls the sensitivity of sculpture from southern Mesopotamia. In this connection, how many monuments have been plundered by conquerors who have afterwards engraved their names upon them? Let us think of Shutruk-Nahhunte of Susa who in the twelfth century BC filled his temples and palace with statues and stelae he found during his conquests in Mesopotamia (Amiet 1988: 98–101). Ashur-bel-kala would not have been the first or the last to do this, and consequently we can suggest that this statue was probably carved in Babylonia one or two centuries before his reign.

9 Drawing of *kudurru* of Nabu-shuma-ishkun, king of Babylon, eighth century BC.

While the kings called Kurigalzu reigned over Babylonia in the fourteenth century, the country of Elam came out of the darkness through the inspiration of king Untash-Napirisha. Thanks to a tablet in Berlin, published in 1986 by Jan van Dijk (1986), we now know that this king of Susa reigned in the fourteenth century and not in the thirteenth century BC, as was hitherto supposed. Thanks to the results of excavations at Susa and Choga Zanbil, the ancient Dûr-Untash, we are in a good position to assess the quality of the art of this period.

The only surviving part of a white limestone statue shows king Untash-Napirisha standing, lifesize, in a long, tight skirt (Pl. 7; Spycket 1981: 309, pl. 199). It is inscribed in two languages, Babylonian and Elamite. Drilled into the stone are a series of regularly spaced small holes. This dotted pattern imitates embroidery, and can also be seen on a fragmentary stone stela of Untash-Napirisha (Amiet 1988: fig. 53) and on the massive bronze statue of Napir-asu, his wife (Amiet 1988: fig. 57). While the king's skirt is quite cylindrical, that of the queen is bell-shaped, perhaps reflecting the technical differences between making sculpture in stone and in metal. The extreme complexity of the garment of Napir-asu is made possible by casting the bronze in the lost-wax method, but some details and the inscription were chiselled after casting. The monument is so well-known that I do not want to spend longer describing it. On account of its size and its weight (1750 kg), it remains a triumph of the metalworker's skill.

A similar garment is worn on a faience statuette from Choga Zanbil (Spycket 1981: 314, pl. 205), but this time the fabric is dotted by circlets (Pl. 8a). The hands are placed on top of each other as on the statue of Napir-asu. In both cases there are thick rings on the wrists, three on the faience statuette, four on the queen. In the same temple of the goddess Pinikir at Choga Zanbil was another female statuette, also headless (Ghirshman 1968: pls VII/7–8, LXIX), and an attractive head (Pl. 8b; Spycket 1981: pl. 203) which does not fit onto any of the bodies and whose sex is uncertain. I think that it is a young man with a haircut similar to that on a small head from Susa (Pl. 9; Spycket 1981: pl. 202), also of faience, ht. 3 cm, which is obviously male with its thick curled hair.

Still on the subject of Elamite clothing, we should remark that the dotted fabric is certainly a fashion of the time of Untash-Napirisha. We see it on two figures carrying kids or young goats in gold and in silver, ht. 7.5 cm (Pl. 10; Amiet 1966: figs 318–9) and on a figure carrying a bird in bronze, ht. 11 cm (Amiet 1966: fig. 315), but some other worshippers wear plain skirts.

A small female statuette, ht. 6 cm, in limestone from Susa, restrainedly carved, wears a long dress covering both shoulders with folded and fringed hems that fall down in flaps (Pl. 11; Spycket 1981: 315, pls 206 a-b). Such a garment is worn by the princess Bar-Uli, daughter of Shilhak-Inshushinak, on a chalcedony bead in the British Museum (Col. Pl. X; Amiet 1966: fig. 340). Thanks to this representation, we can suggest that the lost head of the statuette was covered with a voluminous turban similar to that on a small ivory head, ht. 3.5 cm, from Susa in the Louvre (Pl. 12; Spycket 1981: pl. 207).

A striking feature of Elamite civilisation is the importance of the snake. It was already attested during the Sukkalmah Period at the beginning of the second millennium BC, but is particularly widespread in Middle Elamite sculpture. We see it surrounding the stela of Untash-Napirisha and

10 Drawings of cylinder seals with snake thrones from Susa.

on top of a bronze table carried by five men in high relief holding vases (Amiet 1966: fig. 291). Two snakes' heads cross one another like a diadem on the forehead of a large female head that is broken away beneath the eyes (Pl. 13; Amiet 1966: fig. 290). Sometimes the snake's head is horned as on the throne of a god (Amiet 1966: figs 286A-C). This is also seen on cylinder seals (Fig. 10) from Susa (Amiet 1972: nos 2015–17, 2330) and Haft Tepe (Miroschedji 1981: pl. 7). The throne was made for a statue similar to that which is now represented only by the bust of a figure gripping two horned snakes (Amiet 1966: fig. 289). This god, according to the convincing arguments presented by P. de Miroschedji, must be Inshushinak, god of fertility, rather than Napirisha who was nevertheless the patron god of the king Untash-Napirisha.

Popular Sculpture

Popular sculpture is represented by terracotta figurines. The use of clay, a less expensive material than stone or metal, meant that figurines could be mass produced after the invention of the single mould at the end of the third millennium BC.

It is again 'Aqar Quf which has provided a series of moulded terracottas of the thirteenth-twelfth century BC, accidentally found near the site in 1946 (Mustafa 1947). Five fragments of kneeling men, fully dressed, are specially striking. One of them, minus its head like all these fragments, is inscribed on the back with five lines of cuneiform, unfortunately not deciphered. Other inscriptions from the same series mention Gula the goddess of healing. In her temple at Isin, the German expedition of Professor B. Hrouda discovered in 1978 a kneeling man, ht. 16.5 cm, wearing only a threefold belt (Col. Pl. XI; Hrouda 1991: fig. on p. 223). The broken right arm was extended forward, and the left arm was held behind the back. As proposed by Eva Braun-Holzinger, when first publishing this piece (1981), it was probably an ex-votive offering made in recognition of a person's recovery from illness. She rightly compared the Isin man to the figurines from 'Aqar Quf. The well-observed proportions of these clay statuettes are admirable.

In Assyria, around the fifteenth century BC, a new technique was developed, that of glazed clay. At Nuzi, sculptures were produced covered with a coating of glaze (Starr 1937–9: II, pl. 101). Faience (sometimes called frit) appeared some two centuries later. From Ashur, besides fairly coarsely fashioned female statuettes, there is a small statuette of a man, ht. 8 cm (Andrae 1935:

80–82, pl. 34 e-f), also in faience. He is standing on a base with three steps (4.5 x 6 x 2.5 cm), covered with a whitish glaze which may originally have been coloured (Pl. 14). As the German archaeologist, Andrae, has shown, he may be compared with the figure on a glazed plaque from Ashur (Andrae 1935: 81, fig. 63) who on the basis of an incomplete three-line inscription is identified as coming from Retenu in Syria. The man is bearded and dressed in a cape and a skirt with fringed sides. Andrae dated the plaque to the time of Tukulti Ninurta I in the thirteenth century BC.

During this period, Mesopotamians seem to have taken no more interest in the production of standard moulded terracottas, while in Elam there was an extraordinary increase in manufacture, unparalleled in the region. We cannot here illustrate all the types found at Susa, but only a few significant examples. Although clay was a cheap material and essentially meant for popular use it was sometimes of fine quality.

Whereas in the first half of the second millennium nearly all of the naked women have their hands clasped (Spycket 1992a: pls 60–83), during the Middle Elamite period they increasingly have their hands supporting their breasts (ibid.: pls 112–30). In the same way, the musicians wearing a long mantle (ibid.: pls 92–6) in the earlier period give way to a wide variety of nude lute players with bow legs (ibid.: pls 141–9).

At the beginning of the Middle Elamite period female figurines are graceful, thanks to their thin hips and long legs (Pl. 15). The overall form is clearly delineated in order to give the feeling of sculpture in the round, whereas in fact the relief is fairly low. A terracotta relief disc, purchased by the Iraq Museum in Baghdad (Basmachi 1976: fig. 108), shows two of these long-legged naked women together with two small lute players with bow legs and three apes either seated or standing (Pl. 16). This circular relief seems to me to represent well the artistic values at the beginning of the Middle Elamite period.

At this stage, the women are adorned with several rows of necklaces and they wear on the right shoulder a chain with herringbone pattern that runs diagonally across the chest. They have two, three or four rings on each wrist, and wear anklets. Over wavy hair is laid a braided diadem which juts out above the forehead. Their ornament becomes more and more costly and elaborate and includes a rosette or a star-shaped pendant. The chain turns into a double set upon both shoulders, crossing in a sliding ring between the breasts and separating again under the hands. At the same time the women become more and more plump in appearance, with enormous shoulders and arms, while the hips are deformed resulting in a hypertrophy of monstrous appearance (Pls 17–18; Spycket 1992a: pls 125–30). Paradoxically, the more the shapes are enlarged, the less thick are the figurines. It is interesting to note that it was Loftus who was the first to find these figurines, at Susa in 1852. Consequently, the largest collection of this type of fat naked women is now in the British Museum. Thanks to the cordial kindness of successive Keepers of the Department of Western Asiatic Antiquities, I have had the privilege to see several times the forty or so examples brought back by Loftus.[1] The group was found together in the same place on the site of Susa, as recorded by Loftus. He writes: 'In a trench, twenty-two feet deep [6.70m], at the south-west corner of the great platform, was discovered a collection of about two hundred terracotta figures, the greater number of which were nude representations of the goddess' (Loftus 1857: 378–9).[2]

Besides these naked women, but less numerous and almost always lacking the head, are well-dressed women (Pl. 19). Others hold a naked baby in their arms (Spycket 1992a: pls 131–4). The dress resembles that of queen Napir-asu, often with the dotted fabric characteristic of the time of Untash-Napirisha. These small sculptures are important in their own right but through them we can also form a better idea of the original range of large sculptures.

Funerary Sculpture

By 'funerary sculpture' I mean the figural objects found in graves whose purpose was to accompany the deceased. In this respect again Elam enjoyed its own practices in addition to those customs that were in more general use.

The so-called 'frit masks', generally less than 10 cm across, were in use all over the Ancient Near East, from the Mediterranean coast to Iran around the thirteenth century BC. As far as their places of discovery are known, they come from temples, like at Tell al-Rimah (Oates 1965: 74, pl. 18a; 1966: 125, pl. 34a) and Isin (Hrouda 1981: 67, pls 26–7), or from tombs as at Mari (Parrot 1969: 410–12) and Ugarit (Schaeffer 1933: 106, pl. XI/2). At Mari they were laid on the chest of the dead. At Susa (Pl. 20; Spycket 1992a: 218, pl. 158), we do not know the exact provenance, but at Choga Zanbil they originated from temples. After André Parrot, who concluded that these 'masques énigmatiques' were 'asexual protectors', Edgar Peltenburg in a substantial article (1977) counted about forty examples.

Contrary to what we would expect, terracotta figurines have seldom been found in graves and those few graves that contained them at Susa were child's burials. However, nine faience statuettes of worshippers with cylindrical bodies (Pl. 21; Spycket 1992a: 218, pl. 159) were found on a platform made of two rows of glazed bricks, interpreted as the pavement of a destroyed tomb or of a royal funerary chapel (Harper et al. 1992: 145–6). Six of them carried a bird as an offering. They were found together with two kid-bearers in gold and silver and other precious objects.

A funerary practice peculiar to the Middle Elamite period consisted of depositing in some burials painted heads of unbaked clay. The heads are almost life-size and are presumably images of the deceased, either man or woman. The eyes were made of painted terracotta and were set into the head with bitumen. In the vaulted tombs containing multiple burials not all the skulls had a corresponding painted head. In one of those tombs, R. Ghirshman found fourteen skeletons and only six heads (Col. Pl. XII), from which only two could be saved, one male and one female (Pl. 22; Ghirshman and Steve 1966: 8–9, figs 20–21). Each of them is characteristic of Elamite fashion in the second half of the second millennium BC. The man wears his hair jutting out over his forehead, and the woman's head, ht. 17.5 cm, has the same braided diadem as the naked women described above (Pl. 17). The inlaid eyes are encircled by bitumen. On the ears is red painted ornament.

Similar polychrome heads of unbaked clay have been discovered at the site of Haft Tepe, situated midway between Susa and Choga Zanbil. Two female heads and a mask, probably male, were found not in a tomb but in a workshop (Negahban 1991: 37–9, pl. 24). The elaborate hairstyles of the women (Pl. 23) were held in place by yellow headbands imitating gold and decorated with painted representations of cabochons (polished stones): white and black on one and white and yellow on the other. Here also the eyes, circled with white, are inlaid. Although unbaked, these expressive heads are true examples of Middle Elamite sculpture and they seem to be real portraits, realistic rather than idealistic.

In conclusion, can we speak of a Kassite style and a Middle Elamite style? On the basis of our present knowledge, only Elamite sculpture shows any evidence of originality, if not of homogeneity. It should be noted that Elamite sculpture is especially associated with popular and funerary activities which are absent in the Mesopotamian sphere. However, a royal workshop was certainly in use during the reign of Untash-Napirisha, when the Mesopotamian kingdoms seem to have been more concerned with other things than leaving monuments for posterity.

Notes

1 These figurines have now been listed in Curtis 1993: nos 8–48.
2 Some fragments and a complete figurine of the small type (Pl. VIII: Spycket 1992a: no. 1057) were purchased by the Louvre before 1870 from a private collection. Cf. Spycket 1992a: 169–70, 172–3, nos 1053–62, 1065–8.

Middle Babylonian Art and Contemporary Iran

by Peter Calmeyer
Deutsches Archäologisches Institut, Abteilung Teheran

Babylonia, rather than any of its famous neighbours, has always been considered as the cradle of civilisation in the Ancient Near East. The cuneiform script was invented here, and the Sumero-Babylonian forms of polytheism, literature, architecture and fine art became models throughout the lands of upper Mesopotamia, Syria, Anatolia and Iran. During the third millennium and the first half of the second millennium BC, this cultural domination continued. After the destruction of the Old Babylonian empire, however, some of these neighbours developed strong, centralised kingdoms, independent of each other, partly under the influence of recently arrived immigrants. One of these peoples, the Kassites, became so strong in Babylonia itself that one of their leading families was able to take over the throne. For more than two centuries this 'Kassite dynasty' ruled middle and lower Mesopotamia. Therefore, it should come as no surprise that we find foreign elements in the iconography and style of Mesopotamian art. The development of Middle Babylonian (and Assyrian) art was, no doubt, also influenced by the surrounding, newly created cultures. On the other hand, when we consider whether Babylonian civilisation remained strong enough to influence its neighbours, we are confronted by a number of scholarly difficulties.

The most obvious is that of the chronology. We do not know exactly when the Kassite dynasty came to power, as a long list of royal names in the Babylonian king list may include petty kings of the Kassite tribe outside the country. This uncertainty is also the reason for the problem of the 'long' or 'short' chronology in early Mesopotamian history. The Middle Babylonian period ended with a series of invasions by Aramaean tribes from the surrounding steppes. We possess the names and dates of many Babylonian rulers but very few texts, so we do not know exactly what happened. 'Middle Babylonian' might, therefore, be described as being sandwiched between two Dark Ages.

There is a similar dearth of evidence for art and archaeology at both the beginning and end of the period. Not before the second half of the Kassite dynasty do we feel that we are on safer ground, especially in the sphere of seals. Impressions on numerous tablets from Nippur (Matthews 1992) as well as cylinder seals in various collections allow us to distinguish between Assyrian and Babylonian seals and to establish two distinct late Kassite styles (Matthews 1990). The following period, under the self-styled 'kings of Isin', our so-called Second Dynasty of Isin in the twelfth and eleventh centuries BC, developed a glyptic style of its own. The same three Middle Babylonian stylistic groups are to be found amongst the reliefs on the *kudurru* or 'boundary stones' with texts recording grants of land that are usually very well dated (see Fig. 13).

Due to the uprisings accompanying the Aramaean migrations, there is an almost total lack of dated material in the period after the fall of the Second Dynasty of Isin. Only in the tenth century BC can we determine a pictorial style on *kudurru* and metal vessels (see Figs 19–20) as well as a language and orthography that belong to the Neo-Babylonian age.

Moving on now to relations between Mesopotamia and Iran, the traffic routes between these areas should be reconstructed according to modern conditions, or better still, following the medieval caravan routes about which we are well informed. Contemporary cuneiform itineraries only describe commercial roads from Mesopotamia to the northwest, that is, to Syria and Anatolia. Much later, Neo-Assyrian descriptions of military campaigns through the Zagros repeatedly stress the immense difficulties. Even today these difficulties are easy to comprehend: almost all the mountain chains run parallel to each other from northwest to southeast, and the passes through the peaks are few and narrow. As a field commander wrote to Sargon II, 'the terrain is difficult; it lies between the mountains, the waters are constricted and the current is strong, not fit for using either wineskins or keleks' (Lianfranchi and Parpola 1990: no. 200).

One of the tolerably passable routes extends north-northwest from Babylon, through the later *sanjaq* (district) of Sulaimaniya to northern Kurdistan and on to Lake Urmia. The Sasanians made pilgrimages along this route to the holy fire at Takht-i Suleiman, and valuable Kassite objects must have travelled by this road to Hasanlu.

In Level IVB of this fortress excavated by an American expedition[1] an inlaid stone vessel was found with an inscription of the Kassite king Kadashman-Enlil, the second ruler of that name of the early thirteenth century BC (Pl. 24). A similar frieze of recumbent horned animals alternating with small palmette trees can be seen on two reconstructed glass beakers from the same site (Marcus 1991). These beakers (Fig. 11) were made by fusing together prefabricated elements in different colours: probably red, dark and light blue and perhaps orange. In an admirable article about them, Michelle Marcus (1991) has compared her reconstructions with Babylonian cylinder seals (Fig. 12) and the somewhat later wall paintings from the royal residence of Dur-Kurigalzu, modern 'Aqar Quf near Baghdad. The highly sophisticated technique of such mosaic glass vessels has its counterparts in northern Assyria and at Marlik in northern Iran, a site which we will consider below. These fused glass vessels were luxury goods. On their way from Babylonia to Hasanlu they had to cross Assyria, or at least touch on areas that were within the Assyrian sphere of influence. For these geographical reasons we would in fact expect Assyrian influence to be

11 (left) Reconstruction of mosaic beaker from Hasanlu.

12 (above) Drawing of cylinder seal impression from Tell Subeidi.

much stronger than Babylonian in these northern regions, and that is exactly what the cylinder seals from Hasanlu show (Marcus 1988).[2]

The main stream of Babylonian goods and, subsequently, Babylonian artistic influence, must have used what Ernst Herzfeld has called, rather romantically, 'das Tor von Asien'. This overland route, one of the branches of the famous Silk Road of Late Roman and medieval times, the so-called 'Great Khurasan Road' between Baghdad and the frontiers of the Islamic world,

> united the capital with the frontier towns of the Jaxartes on the borders of China. This, too, is perhaps that which of all the roads is best described. Leaving East Baghdâd by the Khurâsân gate, it went across the plain, passing over numerous streams by well-built bridges, to Hulwân at the foot of the pass leading up to the highlands of Persia. Here it entered the Jibâl province and after a steep ascent reached Kirmânshâh, the capital of Kurdistân. Crossing the Jibâl province diagonally, northeast, the road passed through Hamadân to Ray. From Ray onwards it went almost due east to Kûmis, having the Tabaristân mountains on the left, and the Great Desert on the south, till it entered the province of Khurâsân. (Le Strange 1905: 9)

From there the road went on to China. Exactly the same route was used in the time of Augustus, proof of which is the small itinerary written in Greek by Isidorus of Charax on the Persian Gulf called *Parthian Stations*.

The Asian Gate does not figure under this name in the text of Isidorus but instead the mountain *Oros* (Zagros) appears, marking the boundary of the province of Media. Here, near modern Sar-i Pol-i Zohab, on one of the few easy passes, the importance of the place is marked by four still-preserved rock reliefs of the late third and early second millennium BC (Vanden Berghe and Smekens 1984: 19–21, fig. 1). That these reliefs were visible and known at all times is shown by the fact that much later Darius I copied one of them for his famous rock monument at Bisitun (ibid.: 115, pl. 6). Near Sar-i Pol-i Zohab a late Kassite *kudurru* has recently been excavated (Seidl 1989: 222, pl. 33).

Further along the same road, near Kermanshah, a bronze bowl (Pl. 25; Porada 1965: pl. 18) was allegedly found in a cave along with an inscribed dagger of the twelfth century BC (Pl. 1). Both are now in the British Museum. This story does not deserve much credence, perhaps, since it was told by an art dealer who wanted to make his merchandise more interesting. However, two points can be made in its favour. First, in the early 1930s the word 'Luristan' had not yet become a famous label to be attached to nearly all Near Eastern metal objects on the antiquities market. Secondly, hardly anyone at that time, and certainly no art dealer, would have known that this type of dagger and the decoration on the bowl were to be similarly dated to the twelfth or early eleventh century BC.

Today we can be fairly sure of these dates because there are a number of bronze daggers of the same type inscribed in cuneiform with the names and titles of Babylonian kings and high officials (Calmeyer 1969: 59–65). The royal names are those of Adad-shuma-usur, a late Kassite king, and six members of the Isin II dynasty. Later inscriptions are also to be found on less valuable objects, namely beakers and even arrowheads. Unfortunately all these bronzes were illegally excavated. The above-mentioned label 'Luristan' means only that they first appeared in the bazaars of western Iran. There is no question of these humble objects having been used by royalty or high officials. Perhaps the names and titles indicate that the objects were offered to local sanctuaries, or, rather, to warriors who had served the Babylonians. The custom of giving weapons as honorary gifts is, though much later, well attested in a poem by the Greek poet Alkaios about his brother Antimenidas who was a mercenary: 'From the ends of earth you are come, with your sword-hilt of ivory bound with gold … fighting beside the Babylonians you accomplished a great labour, and delivered them from distress, for you slew a warrior who wanted only one palm's breadth of five royal cubits' (Page 1995: 223).

It is certainly possible that from the late Kassite era onwards the inhabitants of the Zagros mountains often served the Babylonian kings as mercenaries.

The date of the bronze bowl (Pl. 25) is also well established. The sacred tree, here between two bulls, has a special stylised form that makes it a *leitmotif* in the Isin II group of seals first described by Ernst Herzfeld sixty years ago. Trees of the same pattern, with a kind of halo of leaves, are also found on the garments and hats of (probably) Nabu-kudurri-usur I (Fig. 13) and Marduk-nadin-ahhe (back jacket) as seen on their boundary-stones (Seidl 1989: 76, 79). These designs were either woven or embroidered. The sacred tree on the royal garments could have easily reached even remote areas through textiles or on cylinder or stamp seals. Of course, the textiles do not

13 *Kudurru* from Babylon in Walters Art Gallery, Baltimore.

survive, but a bronze finger ring, with a stylised tree between two gazelles (Pl. 26), is such an imported object. The inscription using Sumerian ideograms invokes the protection of the gods. The script can be read only on the ring, as it is worn, and not on the impression where it would have been reversed. While in Mesopotamia and Syria such rings were used for making impressions on cuneiform tablets, in order to seal them, in Iran they were apparently mere amulets.

A large number of cylinder seals (e.g. Pls 27–9) were all found at Surkh Dum-i Luri, a small sanctuary of local character in the middle of the modern province of Luristan. Even today the Kuhdasht plain where the site is situated is a remote area. When it was surveyed and excavated in the late 1930s it was still dangerous and the expedition was robbed. We must be thankful that the records of the excavator and most of the objects were preserved and they have recently been published, nearly thirty years after E.F. Schmidt's death (Schmidt *et al.* 1989). The contents of the sanctuary show that this region – as well as that of Hasanlu – did not use clay tablets for writing. The inscribed objects were imported, for example a seal with an inscription of the Kassite king Kurigalzu II (Brinkman in Schmidt *et al.* 1989: 476, no. 2). Whether anyone was able to read Kurigalzu's votive inscription to the goddess Ninlil is doubtful. Obviously the many cylinders were offered to the gods as precious objects. Whether such objects were sent directly from

Babylonia to the sanctuary, or whether they were first acquired by local people – as gifts or booty – and then given to the deity as votive offerings we do not know. The latter must have been the case with some seals which were more than four hundred years old when they were presented (eg. Pl. 27, in Old Babylonian style). Other seals that were probably roughly contemporary with the cult[3] show a variety of styles and influences. There are several local styles and – not surprising geographically – there is some Elamite influence (Pl. 28).

A special product of the region must have been the type of bronze pin with head hammered into a large flat plaque (Moorey 1971: pls 57–8; Amiet 1976a: nos 187–90; de Clercq-Fobe 1978). At Surkh Dum-i Luri a large number of them were found for the first time in a properly controlled excavation. Some were stuck into the walls of the building, clearly votive offerings, probably for a female deity. The original purpose of these disc-pins, however, must have been practical: they were fastened into the upper parts of garments, as shown on a pin-head also from Surkh Dum-i Luri (Fig. 14). The weight of the heads would have turned the pins upside down, as in this illustration. Both the form of the pins and their use comes from Elam (Amiet 1966: fig. 245B). But at Surkh Dum-i Luri the decoration shows Babylonian influence. The halo of leaves, flowers and buds which often surrounds a central boss in the form of the mask of a lion, a woman or perhaps sometimes a man, is very similar to the Isin II type of sacred tree (e.g. Pl. 30). Simpler pins have these haloes without the head. A face in the same style can be seen with a figure shown frontally on a fragment of pin-head in Zurich (Fig. 15). This obviously represents a goddess between palm(?) trees with two male attendants in typically Babylonian dress (cf. Fig. 13). The style of these disc-shaped pin-heads is local, while the iconography shows two contrasting foreign influences: Elamite, as in the snake goddess in Fig. 14, and Babylonian (Fig. 15, Pl. 30).

The relations between Babylonia and Susiana – the most accessible part of the tripartite, highly complex Elamite empire – form a long history of exchange, economically and culturally.[4] Militarily, Elam threatened Mesopotamia more often than *vice versa*. This was certainly true

during the latter half of the second millennium BC. Elamite art of this period was more independent of Babylonia than ever before or after. This independence has been shown by Agnès Spycket's contribution to this colloquium, and it is shown by the famous temple tower at Choga Zanbil, the construction of which is radically different from that of Mesopotamian ziggurats. A letter recently published by Father van Dijk (1986) proves that marriages between the Kassite and Ige-halkid royal families frequently took place on an equal level. Unfortunately this practice led the latter dynasty to claim the Babylonian throne, which inevitably led to war.

In the twelfth century BC the Elamites were the more successful. They raided large areas of Babylonia and removed many works of art to the temples at Susa where they sometimes received a second inscription, as in the case of the well-known stela of Naramsin, third-millennium king of Akkad. Here, they were excavated by the French mission.

That the Elamites not only collected the glorious ancient works of their famous enemies but also appreciated nearly contemporary Babylonian art is shown by two reliefs also found at Susa. These are two Babylonian stelae which have apparently been decapitated. The top parts, with well-preserved enthroned gods in late Kassite style, were re-erected in Susa, but the figures of the original dedicators, probably kings making supplication to the gods, were carefully removed and in one case, replaced by an Elamite prince of the twelfth century BC (Fig. 16). On the other relief, the secondary figure is unfinished and only the new outline has been prepared.

The re-erection of Naramsin's victory stela implies that the Elamites wanted to triumph over their enemy's triumphs. The removal of Hammurabi's laws from Sippar to Susa should probably

14 (far left) Pin-head from Surkh Dum-i Luri.

15 (left) Fragment of decorated bronze sheet, probably part of a disc-pin, in Rietberg Museum, Zurich.

16 (right) Top of a stela from Susa in Musée du Louvre.

be interpreted to mean that Babylonia would be abandoned to permanent disorder. The two stela heads, on the other hand, must be seen differently. The Susian prince wanted to shift the favour of the alien god to himself and his city. He was to be venerated, and his images appreciated and considered powerful.

On the way between Mesopotamia and Susiana there are no formidable obstacles. The ancient tin-trade, and of course all the military campaigns in both directions, only had to avoid the Zagros chains and the swamps in the south. Between the two regions the city of Dêr, modern Badrah, frequently occurs in military reports. It was here that the fiercest clashes took place during the Iraq-Iran war. But once Khuzistan is reached, of which Susiana is part, there is no easy access to Northern Iran. The natural continuation of the Susa road led to Anshan and at a later period to Persepolis.[5]

Whenever the Babylonians wanted to trade their cereals or luxury goods for the horses of the highlands or the copper and iron of the northern mountains, they had to start at the Asian Gate described above. They had to follow the Great Khurasan Road for two-thirds of its length. Then, from the plain of Qazvin at the southern foot of the Elburz range, the ancient caravans would turn in a northwesterly direction to where the Qyzyl Uzun or Sefid Rud ('Golden' or 'White' River) had over the centuries dug its way through the Elburz. From here both the most important valleys and the fertile coastal plains of the Caspian Sea could be reached.

All this, however, is mere speculation on the basis of modern geographical conditions – or it would be, if we did not have evidence from two excavated sites in this region. The results of one of them are published sufficiently well for tentative conclusions to be drawn. This is Marlik Tepe, excavated in 1961–2 by Ezat O. Negahban in a valley leading to the Sefid Rud. Here fifty-three or more tombs dug into a natural mound contained an incredible wealth of gold, silver and bronze vessels, weapons, some jewellery, a few seals, and the extremely fine pottery of this region. The most spectacular objects were exhibited in Tehran, followed in 1964 by a preliminary report (Negahban 1964).[6]

Following the exhibition and publication of these finds a discussion began about their date, their significance and about the ancient population of the region.[7] Some objects can, with confidence, be dated to the twelfth century BC;[8] others, especially the spouted bronze jars of sophisticated and complex workmanship, may be as late as the eighth century BC (Calmeyer 1969: 99–105). As for the population, we should bear in mind I.M. Diakonoff's warning in a recent volume of the *Cambridge History of Iran*: 'Direct identification of archaeological cultures with ethnolinguistic communities are often extremely risky and unreliable' (Diakonoff 1985: 53–4). Much later, the Greeks knew about the Amardoi, apparently an Iranian tribe, in this region.

The most surprising feature about the Marlik finds is the diversity of style amongst the embossed vessels (Col. Pls XIII-XV; Pl. 31; Fig. 17). Vladimir Lukonin, in whose memory this seminar takes place, recorded the following impression of the exhibition at Tehran:

> Bei genauerer Untersuchung erwies sich, daß, ungeachtet einiger Details in Stil und Technik, die
> sie in eine oder mehrere Gruppen einordneten, die Darstellungen auf diesen Gegenständen

17 Drawing of gold beaker from Marlik with four registers of decoration.

außerordentlich verschiedenartig waren – es sind insgesamt vier Richtungen von Verbindungslinien zu benachbarten Kulturen festzustellen. (Lukonin 1986: 14).[9]

Thanks to the publication of the relief vessels (Negahban 1983) we can now improve on this assessment. In her forthcoming dissertation Ulrike Löw will distinguish seven different stylistic groups.

For our purpose, which is the tracing of Babylonian influence, the most important style is that of seven gold vessels (Negahban 1983: nos 5,7–8, 11–13,15; our Col. Pls XIII-XV, Pl. 31) which are distinguished by their plasticity and realistic detail. In spite of this apparent realism the subjects are mainly monsters and exotic creatures (Col. Pls XIV-XV, Pl. 31). They are firmly connected to Babylonian art, especially to the Isin II style (Pls. 25–6, Fig. 13), by the decoration on their base (Pl. 31) and the form of our *leitmotif*, the sacred tree (Col. Pls XIII–XIV). In Babylonia itself, apart from *kudurru* (Fig. 13) and cylinder seals (Matthews 1990), there is not much to compare them with: the only evidence for such a highly developed toreutic art is a tiny fragment of gold rim with double guilloche from 'Aqar Quf, a residence of the late Kassite kings near Baghdad (Baqir 1945: pl. 27).

These seven gold vessels – probably imported to Marlik – are the most beautiful and best preserved specimens of the whole Isin II style. But they are not the only pieces of highly developed craftsmanship from this site. Apart from a spouted silver jar with inlaid decoration including Assyrianising winged monsters (Negahban 1983: no. 21; 1990) and a gold goblet with two friezes of highly stylised bulls, called by the excavator 'unicorns' (Negahban 1983: no. 9), from an unknown local school of metalworking, the most famous single piece is a gold beaker with four friezes of animal scenes (Negahban 1983: no. 14; here Fig. 17). Its workmanship is perhaps a little less sophisticated: the low relief, the animals with patterned bodies and the tendency to fill the available space with figures, point to a non-Mesopotamian, most probably western Iranian, workshop.

The friezes on this beaker have frequently been described as scenes out of the life of a goat. That is not quite correct, but there can be no doubt that they have to be 'read' from bottom to top. In the lowest register is a short-tailed animal with its young suckling. The animal, with hoofs but lacking horns, is perhaps a deer, but certainly not a goat. It is repeated five times. The motif - not the style – occurs on Kassite seals (Matthews 1990: no. 182 – cow) and Middle Assyrian seals (Matthews 1990: 359 – sheep). It is also found on a cylinder seal from the central part of Luristan, acquired by members of the Surkh Dum-i Luri expedition (Pl. 32). In the next register up, the animals standing on either side of a sacred tree, repeated four times, are a very popular motif in Late Kassite and Isin II glyptic art (Matthews 1990). Again, however, they seem to copy the subject, but not the style. G. N. Kurochkin (1990), who has treated thoroughly all the motifs on our beaker, prefers to derive the goats in the tree from the somewhat earlier Mitanni glyptic which could be true since the so-called 'common style' of Mitannian origin did indeed reach Marlik (Pls 33–4). Nevertheless the composition of the whole scene, especially the upright posture of the animals eating the plant's youngest sprouts, is characteristically Babylonian. The form of the tree is, so far as we know, unique; far from any natural prototype, it must be a west Iranian invention. The hyenas and the birds of prey in the third frieze have a threatening meaning. In the fourth, uppermost register the final catastrophe has come upon the world of the herbivorous animals: vultures are devouring a gazelle. Similar groups sometimes appear as accessory scenes on seal impressions from Nippur, for instance on the seal of the son of a certain Kurigalzu, possibly the second Kassite king of that name, around 1300 BC (Fig. 18).

Consequently, we should not speak of scenes out of the life of a goat, or of one animal. It is, however, a matter of life and death, so striking and, I think, so moving, that one cannot avoid speculating about the religion or philosophy which lay behind it. Because this beaker came to light in Iran, one is tempted to think of Zarathustra and his endless struggle between good and evil, between good and bad animals.

However, the invasion of Iranian tribes into present-day Iran happened during one of the darkest ages of the Ancient Near East and whether some or all of those tribes were followers of

18 Drawing of cylinder seal impression from Nippur.

19 *Kudurru* in British Museum re-used in time of
Nabu-mukin-apli.

Zarathustra, we do not know. Hence we should not speculate too much. We should be content
with the statement that the motifs in this cycle of life and death come from Babylonia – and we
should remind ourselves that this theme had long been part of Mesopotamian religious and epic
literature.

It is often assumed that the Isin II style was not confined to the dynasty of that name, but
continued well into the tenth century BC. This erroneous notion is based on the presence of our
leitmotif on a *kudurru* (Fig. 19) with a text from the time of king Nabu-mukin-apli (as late as *c.*950
BC). It has always been overlooked that the relevant designs on the royal garment are part of an old
relief, partly erased but reused with new figures and inscription (Seidl 1965: 186).[10] The style of
the new figures and also of the king's face is that of the tenth century BC.

This conclusion is corroborated by inscriptions of Babylonian officials of the same period on
some of the bronze beakers with pointed bottoms, sometimes called 'situlae' (Calmeyer 1973).
Almost all of these come from the art market, and are allegedly 'from Luristan'. One piece
undoubtedly comes from southern Babylonia. Only four fragments have been excavated by
scholars, at Surkh Dum-i Luri (Schmidt *et al.* 1989: 321–2, pls 190 f-g, 204 b-c). The style is that
of the *kudurru* of the tenth century, with grotesque faces and floating outlines.

With these objects we have gone beyond the Middle Babylonian or Middle Elamite era. Yet it was necessary to consider them for two reasons. Firstly, the tenth century BC is the last period when Babylonia was in a position to influence western Iran. In the ninth century BC the growing new power, the Neo-Assyrian empire, acquired the province of Bit Namri, just in front of the Asian Gate. As Assyria became dominant, only Assyrian inscriptions and Assyrianising objects could enter western Iran. The other reason is that one of these 'situlae' bears a unique decorative scene, which is an illustration out of the Babylonian national epic (Fig. 20). Gilgamesh and his friend Enkidu are shown slaying the monster Humbaba. Gilgamesh wears the slightly old-fashioned outfit of Babylonian royalty, and Enkidu has the curly hair of a half-civilised creature from the steppes. Nothing could express better the proud attitude of the Babylonians, based on a tradition of two millennia, especially their pretension to dominate the unruly, the wild and the monstrous.

20 Decoration on bronze beaker showing scene from the Gilgamesh epic.

Notes

1 For a recent survey of these excavations, see Dyson and Voigt 1989.

2 See also Winter 1977.

3 The chronology of the Surkh Dum sanctuary is problematic. The excavators recorded a few late cylinder seals beneath floors, i.e. predating the deposits of Phases 2C and 2B respectively above those floors (Schmidt *et al.* 1989: 448, 488, nos 51 and 204). On the other hand, the overwhelming majority of the objects apparently belong to the late second millennium BC. There are several possible solutions, none of them satisfactory. First, there might be a problem with the stratigraphy, but the excavation was apparently carried out very carefully and it would be churlish to criticise an excavation that took place sixty years ago. In the case of seal no. 51 perhaps the whole group should be dated earlier than is usually done; similar seals from Hasanlu IVB must be much older than the current date of '*c.*800 BC'. Phase 2B, ending around 600 BC, perhaps existed for a long time and kept many heirlooms.

4 This history has recently been the subject of a Rencontre Assyriologique. See De Meyer and Gasche 1991. For surveys of the archaeology and history of Elam see Carter and Stolper 1984.

5 Trade with eastern Iran was always in Elamite hands; actually, it might have been the *raison d'être* of the Elamite state. It is only in recent years that it has become clear to us that, from the Early Bronze Age onwards, the low plains of Khuzistan had interchange with most of the 'upper countries', as far as Bactria (northern Afghanistan and Tadjikistan) and the border of the Indian sub-continent. See Amiet 1986.

6 For later reports, see Negahban 1968; 1977; 1983; 1990.

7 See also Amiet 1990.

8 See, e.g., the contents of Tomb XVIIB, as drawn by C. Wolff in Calmeyer 1982: pl. 39. This drawing does not, incidentally, contain all the objects from the tomb.

9 For similar views, see Calmeyer 1973: 203ff, and Calmeyer 1982.

10 This ugly *kudurru* deserves much more attention than it has hitherto received.

Excavations in Luristan and Relations with Mesopotamia

by Louis Vanden Berghe† and Alexander Tourovets
Gent and Brussels

Within the framework of this seminar we intend to consider some aspects of the excavations in the Pusht-i Kuh, Luristan, and to examine the relations between Luristan and Mesopotamia, especially Assyria, during the Iron Age III period, that is *c.*800–600 BC. Between 1965 and 1979 the Belgian Archaeological Expedition conducted fifteen campaigns of survey and excavation in the Pusht-i Kuh. These excavations have resulted in the discovery of a great number of cemeteries covering a long span of time, from the Chalcolithic Period to the end of Iron Age III (*c.*4200–600 BC). In view of the chronological limits fixed for this seminar, however, we must focus our attention on the Iron Age (*c.*1250–600 BC), and this is the period that will be taken into account here when comparing archaeological material from the excavations in the Pusht-i Kuh and from Mesopotamia and Assyria.

The most interesting period is Iron Age III (*c.*800–600 BC) when comparisons can be made with the most valuable results. As a matter of fact, excavations at sites of Iron Age I and II (*c.*1250–800 BC), for example at Bard-i Bal, Kutal-i Gulgul and elsewhere have yielded very little material that is comparable with Mesopotamia. There are only some daggers and swords with the hilt terminating in a more or less developed fan-shaped pommel that can be compared with those depicted on the Assyrian reliefs or examples that have been recovered from archaeological sites in Babylonia and Assyria (Vanden Berghe 1970: 14, fig. 8; 1971: 18, fig. 10; 1973a: fig. on p. 25). By contrast, excavations at Iron Age III sites have made this period very well known and have produced large quantities of material from more than 600 tombs. The most important results have been obtained at the sites of War Kabud, Djub-i Gauhar and Chamzhi Mumah. A large part of this material bears comparison with that recovered from Mesopotamia and particularly from Assyrian sites or depicted on Assyrian reliefs.

The pottery found in tombs of the Iron Age III sites is never painted, the only decoration consisting of finger-nail impressions, incised grooves of various length, or raised knobs. This pottery can be divided into three groups. The first consists of coarse hand-made pottery, buff or yellowish-brown in colour. There are simple forms with a rounded base. The second group comprises a finer wheel-made ceramic which is beige, sometimes tending towards a pinkish colour. There is a variety of quite elaborate forms, often on a flat base. The third group is represented by a very fine ware, greyish black in colour, carefully polished and also wheel-made. There are sometimes incised triangles or concentric circles around the vessels. Some ceramic forms from the Iron Age III cemeteries can be compared with pottery from Assyrian and Neo-Babylonian period sites, such as the pear-shaped or quasi pear-shaped vessels belonging to our third group (Pl. 35). Outside Luristan similar examples have been found at Ashur in Neo-Assyrian levels (Haller 1954: pl. 3c, l, p, y), at Babylon in the Neo-Babylonian period (Strommenger 1964: 169, fig. 9/6) and they are clearly depicted on some Neo-Assyrian reliefs. It is notable that a glazed jar of ovoid form with a tall flaring neck found at War Kabud can be compared with examples found at Ashur (Andrae 1977: 185, fig. 164) and Zincirli (Andrae 1943: 49, pl. 22 b,c). In the Iron Age III sites, animal-shaped vessels have been found at War Kabud, Chamzhi Mumah and Djub-i Gauhar (Pl. 36). These vessels are characterised by cylindrical bodies with a funnel-shaped spout on the back. Bulls and goats are the most common.

As for metalwork in bronze and iron, it can be observed that during the Iron Age III period weapons such as daggers, swords, spearheads, arrowheads, axes and adzes as well as tools are made exclusively of iron. Among the swords and daggers two types can be identified. The first group (Pl. 37; Vanden Berghe 1968: pl. 27c) consists of swords and daggers with the hilt covered in bronze sheet and terminating in a crescent-shaped pommel. Sometimes the bronze sheet is held in place by bronze studs. The second group (Pl. 38; Vanden Berghe 1968: pl. 27b) comprises swords and daggers with the tang terminating in a bronze button. On Assyrian reliefs these types of weapon are not exactly represented as the pommels and hilts of swords and daggers on the reliefs are generally more complex and elaborate. There are only a few illustrations of daggers like those recovered from Luristan. The best comparisons are to be found on reliefs from the reigns of Sargon II and Sennacherib, and perhaps also Ashurbanipal, showing mainly but not exclusively tribute and booty from captured cities in foreign countries. In contrast to the Assyrian reliefs, numerous illustrations of similar types of sword and dagger with crescent-shaped pommels are to be found in Syro-Hittite art of the second half of the ninth and also of the eighth century BC, for example at Zincirli and Carchemish (Bittel 1976: figs 259, 300, 303). As far as other types of weapon are concerned, we should mention axes and adzes, spearheads and arrowheads. Naturally, the more common weapons with leaf-shaped blades are found at several sites in Assyria and Babylonia.

If iron was used exclusively for weapons and tools, so bronze was used for ceremonial objects, personal ornaments and luxury vessels, as well as for applied decoration, for example on hilts. Amongst the ceremonial weapons, which may sometimes have been used also as real weapons, we should mention maceheads, shields, quivers and axe-adzes.

Bronze maceheads were often found placed in tombs together with a shield. They were not only used as weapons as depicted on some war reliefs of Ashurbanipal,[1] but were probably also sceptre-heads, ceremonial weapons that served as symbols of rank as can be seen on a great number of Assyrian reliefs from various reigns. The majority of the maceheads from our excavations in Luristan have a cylindrical or quasi-cylindrical shaft sometimes reinforced at both ends with ribs. This ribbed decoration on the shaft seems to be characteristic of the Iron Age III period. Near the upper end is generally a globular or bulbous swelling. Amongst these maceheads there are a number of different types from the Iron Age III cemeteries but unfortunately only four of these types are comparable to those depicted on the Assyrian reliefs.[2]

The first type recovered from the tombs of the Pusht-i Kuh (Pl. 39, right) is a macehead with a plain globular or bulbous swelling two-thirds of the way up the shaft. This represents the simplest and most common form even though some pieces show the bulbous part nearer the top of the shaft. Occasionally this upper part is surmounted by three or more projections or spikes. This form of macehead is depicted on Assyrian reliefs from those of Ashurnasirpal II (883–59 BC) in the North-West Palace at Nimrud to those of Sargon II (721–705 BC) at Khorsabad. The same form also occurs on Neo-Hittite wall slabs at Carchemish dating from the end of the ninth century BC. One of these depicts king Yariris holding a macehead of this type (Hogarth 1969: pl. B7a). And at Arslan Tash some of the reliefs from the palace of Tiglath-pileser III (744–27 BC) show soldiers holding such maceheads (Thureau Dangin et al. 1931: pls. 8–9). Similar examples in bronze have been discovered at Khorsabad and in bronze and iron from Nimrud and Zincirli (Andrae 1943: 88, figs 105, 107i). Recently John Curtis published some interesting maceheads found at Sherif Khan (ancient Tarbisu) where bronze and iron are also combined in the bulb (Curtis and Grayson 1982: fig. 1/1–3, pls 3a-b). These forms recall the examples with globular bulb from our excavations in the Pusht-i Kuh.

The second group consists of maceheads where the bulbous part is decorated with vertical ribs (Pl. 39, centre). They are sometimes called 'melon shaped' (Moorey 1971: 92–5). Similar maceheads seem to be depicted on reliefs from Tiglath-pileser III's palace at Arslan Tash, and also, but of slightly earlier date, at Carchemish (Hogarth 1914: pl. B5). The excavations at Zincirli have produced an isolated example of this type of macehead which seems to be less common outside Luristan (Andrae 1943: fig. 107l, pl. 42l).

The third group is characterised by maceheads in the form of a rosette (Pl. 40; Vanden Berghe 1968: pl. 30d). These pieces can be compared to examples shown on reliefs from the North-West Palace of Ashurnasirpal II at Nimrud (Madhloom 1970: pl. XXXI/16). During the following reigns they seem to be depicted less often, and their scarcity is perhaps reflected by the fact that no examples have been found in Assyria.

There is a last group represented by pieces with a bulbous swelling with several rows of knobs (Pl. 39, left). This type seems to be the same as that represented on wall paintings of the palace of Tiglath-pileser III at Til Barsip (Thureau-Dangin 1930: pl. 23; Thureau-Dangin and Dunand 1936: pl. 49).

As far as we know, the only bronze quiver plaque found in Luristan during controlled excavations comes from the site of War Kabud. This bronze sheet is divided by horizontal bands decorated with dotted circles into three large but irregular registers containing rosettes (Pl. 41; Vanden Berghe 1968: pl. 29c). The numerous holes on the edges of this plaque show that it was once sewn onto a leather frame. Similarly decorated quivers are depicted on many Assyrian reliefs between the reigns of Ashurnasirpal II and Ashurbanipal, especially on those showing war scenes. Other quivers from illegal excavations in the Pusht-i Kuh, mainly in the region of Ilam and Gilan Gharbi near the Iraqi border, have designs which are reminiscent of Assyrian art. Those found during clandestine digging in the Pish-i Kuh (east of the Pusht-i Kuh), on the other hand, have typically Luristan iconographic motifs which are also found, for example, on the votive pins from Surkh Dum-i Luri.[3]

Shields have been recovered from tombs at War Kabud, Tatulban, Djub-i Gauhar and Chamzhi Mumah. All the shields are circular in shape and have a projecting conical boss in the centre (Pl. 42). Occasionally there are one or more concentric circles in repoussé at regular intervals around this central boss. There are pierced holes on opposite sides in the outer edge of the shield. The existence of such holes may indicate that the shields were originally fixed to wicker or leather frames. The shields are more or less of the same size, with diameters varying from 27 cm to 32 cm. Contrary to what is generally believed, they were not just the central parts or discs fixed onto large wooden or leather shields, but they were used as shields by themselves. In fact, nearly identical small round shields with turned up edges and central boss are depicted on reliefs from the reign of Ashurnasirpal II and also on the bronze strips of the wooden gates of Shalmaneser III from Balawat. Also during the ninth century, shields of a similar type were carved on basalt orthostats at Tel Halaf (Pritchard 1954: pl. 164). We cannot exclude the possibility that similar shields were used in Assyria during the eighth and seventh centuries BC, but those shown on the reliefs generally seem to be larger than our examples from Luristan.

As for the bronze axe-adzes found in our excavations we have not been able to find any comparable examples either on the reliefs or amongst the archaeological material from Meso-potamia. On the upper parts of our examples there are sometimes human heads in relief on both sides of the shaft (Vanden Berghe 1987: fig. 20). These objects have no practical use on account of the accentuated curve of the blades and the narrow diameter of the socket and therefore of the haft. The representation of the human head on the collar indicates with little doubt that these objects had a votive significance. In our view these are typical Luristan bronzes as to the best of our belief no similar items have ever been discovered outside Luristan.

A great variety of sheet bronze vessels occurred in the Iron Age III cemeteries in the Pusht-i Kuh, Luristan. Sometimes incised geometric and figural designs can be seen on these vessels. Each tomb belonging to a person of important social status contained a bronze bowl which was usually placed on a large pottery jar or on a pot with tubular spout. In more humble burials this bronze item was replaced by a pottery cup or bowl. The most common and simplest form of bronze bowl is an open hemispherical type found at all sites. It is also represented on Assyrian reliefs and at Assyrian sites, and is therefore not especially typical for Luristan. More interesting are the bowls with central omphalos. These vessels have a flat base with a rosette chased in the centre around the small omphalos. A bowl from Chamzhi Mumah (Pl. 43) has a decorative frieze consisting of an incised hunting scene arranged around a central rosette. This scene depicts two bowmen each kneeling in a shooting position, their arrows pointed in the direction of a mountain goat. The head of the goat is turned toward the hunter. This composition recalls some of the hunting scenes depicted on 'situlae' (beakers) and votive pins from Luristan (Frankfort 1954: 208, fig. 102; Calmeyer 1969: pls III/2,5, VII/3). The execution of the incised designs is reminiscent of decoration on the Ziwiye and Nimrud ivories.

There are also carinated bowls with a hammered tongue pattern on the bulge and an engraved guilloche pattern between two bands of chevrons on the vertical shoulder. This guilloche design appears on Mesopotamian works from the middle of the second millennium BC but it is most widespread in the first half of the first millennium BC. One can find this motif on the Nimrud ivories and on stone reliefs from Carchemish, as well as on 'situlae' from Luristan (Woolley 1952: B38-B42; Reade 1983: fig. 41; Frankfort 1954: 102, fig. 39, pl. 167c). We found such bowls with bulbous profile and slightly turned out neck at Djub-i Gauhar, Chamzhi Mumah and War Kabud. This shape is typical of an Assyrian workshop (Howes Smith 1986: 48–55). These bowls are depicted on many reliefs from Nimrud where some bronze examples were also found (Mallowan 1966: I, 116, fig. 59). Similar vessels have been found at Ashur (Haller 1954: pl. 22c; Andrae 1977: 186, fig. 165) and also at Zincirli (Andrae 1943: 118, fig. 15, pl. 56 d-e). In both cases they date from the eighth century BC.

Also from Iron Age III sites are the gadrooned bowls, often with a flat base and slightly concave profile. They are decorated with narrow radiating lobes or gadroons hammered in repoussé. Some vessels are decorated with a multi-petalled rosette in the centre surrounded by concentric circles. These bowls decorated with gadroons are often shown on the Assyrian reliefs, for example in royal banquets. Very similar types of vessel have been found in excavations at Ashur and Nimrud and date from the eighth century BC (Haller 1954: pl. 12h; Mallowan 1966: II, fig. 357).

A bowl from Chamzhi Mumah is decorated with chased designs consisting of two broad horizontal bands on the upper part of the vessel (Vanden Berghe 1987: fig. 14/21). That at the top has several layers of superimposed half circles producing a scale-like pattern that in Ancient Near Eastern art is often a schematic representation of mountainous landscape. The second register shows a row of inverted palmettes. The scale-like mountain motif appears frequently on Assyrian reliefs, particularly on scenes of warfare and on the bronze bands from the Balawat Gates of Shalmaneser III. The inverted palmette motif can be found on reliefs with various themes throughout the whole period of Neo-Assyrian and Neo-Babylonian art.

A pyxis from War Kabud (Pl. 44; Markoe 1985: pl. IIIa) has incised decoration representing Assyrian-type fortresses alternating with four winged sphinxes shown in profile. These hybrid figures have human heads, bird breasts, eagle claws and scorpion tails. The decoration on this pyxis brings to mind some figures on Nimrud ivories in Syrian style dating from the ninth and eighth centuries BC (Barnett 1975: 83–5).[4] The fortresses recall the representations of strongholds and walled cities on many Assyrian war reliefs and on the bronze bands from the Balawat Gates. Hence the decoration on this pyxis is very likely to be Assyrian work.[5]

Equally important is the discovery of a bronze bucket with a basket handle (Markoe 1985; Vanden Berghe 1987: fig. 14/23). This vessel is cylindrical in shape with a flat bottom and has a basket handle attached to the body by two cross-shaped attachments rather like highly stylised birds. Around the outside is incised a scene of war, some details of which are unfortunately obscure. One can identify a fortress of nearly the same type as that we have seen on the pyxis from War Kabud, a horse-drawn chariot, archers and a file of prisoners. The nature of this scene and many elements of the decoration are indicative of an Assyrian origin, but some features seem to derive from Iran.[6] As for the form of this bronze vessel, similar buckets occur in many ritual scenes on the Assyrian reliefs throughout the whole period of Neo-Assyrian art, but generally there are differences in the system of attachment. The system on our piece seems to be specifically linked to the attachments depicted on ritual reliefs from the Palace of Ashurnasirpal II at Nimrud and others from the Palace of Sargon II at Khorsabad (Madhloom 1970: pl. LXXXV/6–9, 11; Dyson 1957: figs 3–4, 6; Frankfort 1954: pl. 83).

During our excavations we found a number of vessels with double-ridged profile (Vanden Berghe 1987: fig. 14/24–6). On these vessels there are two convex bulges on the side. The type was discovered in several Iron Age III cemeteries in Luristan but it does not seem to be depicted on the Assyrian reliefs. We can only refer to some bronze examples from Susa and from Neo-Babylonian levels at Uruk (Strommenger 1967: pls. XXXII/7–8, XLVIII/4, XLIX/5). In the last case, the vessels may be imports from Iran (Muscarella 1988a: 260–2).

Of particular importance are the tall cylindrical 'situlae' or goblets with slightly concave sides and rounded bottoms terminating in a nipple base (Pl. 45; Vanden Berghe 1968: pl. 31a, left). The same undecorated bronze 'situlae' have been discovered in Mesopotamia at Uruk (Strommenger 1967: pls. XXXII/5–6, XLIX/1–3), at Mari (in a Neo-Assyrian tomb), at Ashur, at Ur and recently at Haradum (Kepinski and Lecomte 1985: fig. on p. 55). A beaker with tall flared neck and bulbous body terminating in a button or nipple base has also been found (Vanden Berghe 1987: fig. 14/30). Around the base is a rosette centred on the button. A similar vessel in silver has been recovered from Fort Shalmaneser at Nimrud (Mallowan 1966: II, fig. 356).

The discovery of a strainer at Chamzhi Mumah (Pl. 46) is of great interest. This bronze vessel consists of a small cup with a funnel-shaped base and a long handle rising up from the rim. At the base of the cup is a perforated plate filter. Similar strainers have been found in Mesopotamia, for example at Mari in a Neo-Assyrian tomb (Parrot 1952: 188–9, pl. XVII/1). Similar vessels are depicted on Assyrian religious reliefs but there, curiously, the handle is inclined downwards (Hrouda 1965: pl. 52/2).

In the Iron Age III period, fibulae replaced the straight pins. In fact, on all sites and cemeteries of this period we have found only a few pins of the simple form. On the other hand, twenty-three fibulae have been recovered from seven different cemeteries. These fibulae are mostly of the triangular or elbow variety (Pl. 47), but exceptionally there is one with a semicircular bow (Pl. 48; Vanden Berghe 1968: pl. 36b). These fibulae are of the same type as those found in Mesopotamia and Syria and date on the whole to the eighth and seventh centuries BC. The pins of the fibulae were made separately and inserted into a socket at the end of the bow. Generally these pins are in bronze but in two cases they were made of iron. The fibulae have ribbed mouldings on each side of the bow. In an important study David Stronach has classified Near Eastern fibulae according to their shape (Stronach 1959), and our pieces from the Pusht-i Kuh fit easily into his classification. Thus our triangular-shaped fibulae belong to his Group III, 7 and our semi-circular example to his Group I, 5. This last type is clearly depicted on Neo-Hittite reliefs and statuary of the ninth and eighth centuries BC at Marash and Carchemish (Bittel 1976: fig. 317; Woolley 1952: pl. B64c). It is noteworthy that triangular fibulae have been found in excavations at Assyrian sites including Nimrud, Ashur and Khorsabad, and in Neo-Babylonian levels at Nippur and Babylon.

The rings, bracelets and anklets are of very simple form, sometimes engraved or incised just with simple geometric decoration. This is important because it proves that rings, bracelets and anklets decorated with animal designs must be dated earlier than Iron Age III, since none have been found in tombs of this period.

Precious metals such as gold and silver were used for jewellery, especially earrings and spiral hair-rings, in typical Assyrian style. The silver earrings found in the Pusht-i Kuh are pendant-shaped forms of which two types are distinguishable (Pl. 49; Vanden Berghe 1968: pl. 37b). The first type comprises earrings with an annular holder to which is attached a long rod ending in a conical tip decorated with granulation. This type is represented on many Assyrian reliefs and sculptures, sometimes in more elaborate form. An example of nearly the same type as our pieces has been discovered in a tomb at Nimrud but here the pendant is made of rock-crystal (Maxwell Hyslop 1971: pl. 219). The second type consists of an annular ring from which hangs a pendant like a pomegranate or a bunch of grapes made up from large, crude granules. This form is also represented on Assyrian reliefs between the ninth and seventh century BC. Crescent or boat-shaped earrings in gold have been found at only two sites, War Kabud and Dum Shaft Palyah. This form occurs in Late Assyrian levels at sites like Ur, Ashur and Nimrud, but most of these earrings are more elaborate with decorative granulation.

In conclusion, we have been able to establish that the archaeological material from the Iron Age III sites in the Pusht-i Kuh, Luristan, has many features in common with material from Meso-potamia and especially from Assyria. This is mostly the case with bronze objects, including weapons such as maceheads, quivers, shields, and with some types of sword and dagger. Metal vessels can also be compared with those found in Mesopotamia or depicted on Assyrian reliefs. However, there are many bronze objects from Luristan of Iron Age III date which are not known in Mesopotamia, and we are able to say that axe-adzes, master-of-animals standards with supports and some vessels are typical products of Luristan. The relationship between the objects found in the cemeteries of the Pusht-i Kuh and those depicted on Assyrian reliefs or discovered in Mesopotamia raises several imporant questions. Are the Assyrian-like objects found in Luristan cemeteries imports from Mesopotamia or simply local works made by Assyrian craftsmen? Or, are these objects made by local people under strong Assyrian artistic influence? Another possi-bility, but destinctly less plausible, is that the objects depicted or discovered in Assyria came directly from Luristan or were made under the artistic influence of Luristan. In any case, the question of the significance of such discoveries in Iron Age III tombs in Luristan remains largely open. To conclude this paper, however, we can emphasize the impact of Assyrian influence on Luristan indicated by the discovery of a rock carving at Shikaft-i Gulgul probably showing king Esarhaddon worshipping the deities of Assyria.[7]

Notes

1 Assyrian reliefs do not generally show maceheads being used as weapons, but a notable exception is on the reliefs showing the battle of the River Ulaï exhibited in the British Museum.

2 A detailed list of all the types of weapons, especially maceheads, found during excavations in the Pusht-i Kuh, Luristan, is published in Vanden Berghe 1979.

3 See the catalogue of votive pins published in Schmidt *et al.* 1989.

4 Comparisons with the Nimrud ivories are very interesting but the scorpion tail of the War Kabud piece seems to be exceptional.

5 For Muscarella (1988a: 255) this object shows mixed influence because although the style and motifs are essentially Assyrian the iconography seems to be of Iranian origin.

6 Beside questions about the significance of this scene for the history of this region of Luristan and the significance of the occurrence of this vessel in an Iron Age III tomb, the main problem relates to the origin of the vessel. As we have said, the style looks Assyrian but some iconographic elements seem to be of local or Iranian origin. G. Markoe emphasises that the frontal position of the prisoners points to an Iranian rather than an Assyrian origin. Also, the decoration at top and bottom of two bands of stylised cable ornament with a series of oval shapes linked together is most probably of Iranian origin. For a detailed discussion of the scene and the origin of the different iconographic elements see Markoe 1985.

7 This rock carving was discovered by L. Vanden Berghe during the year 1971–2 and first published in Vanden Berghe 1973b: pls 13–14a.

Media and Mesopotamia: History and Architecture[1]

by Michael Roaf
OXFORD

Geography

There could hardly be a greater contrast than that between Media and Mesopotamia, both in their geography and in their history. The Mesopotamian plains are low-lying and flat, completely flat in the alluvial plains of Babylonia, slightly more rolling in Assyria (Col. Pl. XVI). On the other hand Media is more than 1000 m above sea-level and is divided by high mountain ridges which reach over 3000 m (Figs 21–22, Col. Pl. XVII). The mountains of western Iran, the Zagros mountains, consist of a succession of ranges running from the northwest to the southeast forming linked series of mountain valleys, in which the settlements are situated today as in the past. The steep bare mountain slopes can sometimes provide pasture for hardy sheep, goats, donkeys and horses but the agricultural wealth of the region lies in the more fertile valleys. In this mountainous region there is sufficient rainfall to allow cereal crops to grow without irrigation, but this is counterbalanced by the cruel cold of the winter in Media. As one moves towards the central deserts of Iran the rainfall diminishes so that agriculture is only possible where there are springs or canals. These regions are now watered by qanats but there is no certain evidence that qanats were in use in Iran as early as the first half of the first millennium BC.

The limit of rainfed cereal agriculture cuts across northern Mesopotamia. South of this line agriculture is only practicable with the use of irrigation, and where there is no irrigation the land reverts to steppe or desert. Even in regions with sufficient rainfall for cereals the use of irrigation may increase yields and allow the cultivation of other crops which need more water, such as vegetables.

The boundaries of Mesopotamia, except at the northeast, are largely determined by geography. It stretches from the head of the Gulf; to the southwest it is bordered by the sterile deserts of

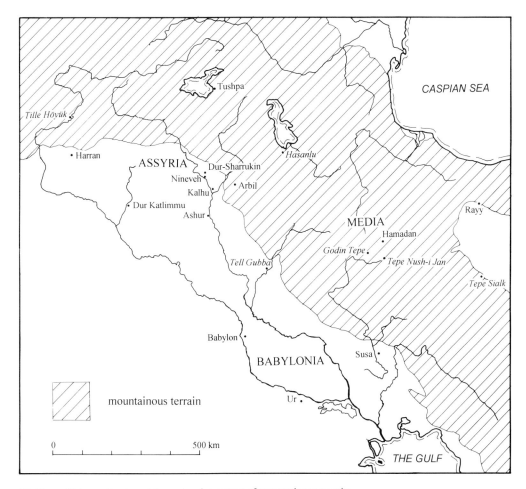

21 Map of Mesopotamia and Iran, showing extent of mountainous terrain.

Arabia and Syria; to the southeast the edge of the Mesopotamian plain is marked by the last ripples of the Zagros mountains; to the northeast, however, the edge of Mesopotamia is less well defined. Mesopotamia is divided into two main regions named after the empires that ruled them, Babylonia in the south and Assyria in the north. Successive Mesopotamian conquerors, once they had united Babylonia and Assyria, expanded their rule over Elam, the lower lying land to the southeast, or into Syria, along the corridor running northwest up the Euphrates and Tigris Rivers and on towards the Mediterranean. This formed a repetitive pattern of early Mesopotamian history seen in the Uruk period and repeated by the kings of Agade, and above all by the Assyrians, but for the most part Mesopotamian rulers did not attempt to conquer the mountainous regions to the north and east.

For two reasons the extent of ancient Media is less well-defined: first we have virtually no information about its northern and eastern borders, though its southern border lay in modern Luristan and to the west it approached Mesopotamia; and second the boundaries of Media

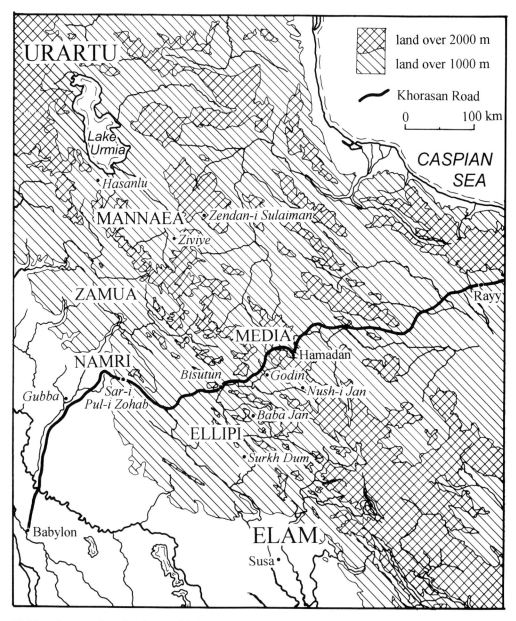

22 Map of western Iran showing possible locations of Media and neighbouring regions in the Late Assyrian period.

changed greatly during the first millennium (Fig. 23). The core of Media, however, lay along the Great Khurasan Road, the part of the famous Silk Route, which led from the Iranian plateau through the Zagros mountains down to Baghdad and the plains of Mesopotamia (Fig. 22). On this important route lay the city of Hagmatana, known to the Greeks as Ecbatana, and now called Hamadan, which was the capital of the Median kingdom in the sixth century BC.

Travel is relatively easy along the lines of the parallel valleys in the Zagros, which run from northwest to southeast, but it is much more difficult to cut across the mountain ranges. In the whole length of the Zagros from Lake Urmia to the Gulf there are only a limited number of routes which are suitable for either trade or invasion. Most of these are difficult routes which follow the various tributaries of the Tigris and climb arduous passes, eventually arriving on the Iranian plateau, but apart from the Great Khurasan Road none of these are suitable for large armies on the march, even though they were on occasion used by the military might of Assyria. The region to the southeast of the Khurasan Road (modern Luristan) was and is equally impenetrable from the lowlands; but travelling along the valleys one can reach the plains of Susiana and from there get to central Mesopotamia along the eastern edge of the Mesopotamian plains.

Within Mesopotamia there were no major obstacles to travel. The Tigris and Euphrates rivers and the network of canals between them offered easy routes for the bulk transport of goods. Rivers, canals and marshes presented some difficulties for those on foot or on animal-back but normally they could be crossed by bridges or ferries or avoided by taking a detour.

The Evidence from Mesopotamia: History

By the end of the second millennium BC Mesopotamia had a continuous history which had developed over some two thousand years and before that its prehistory stretched back into the

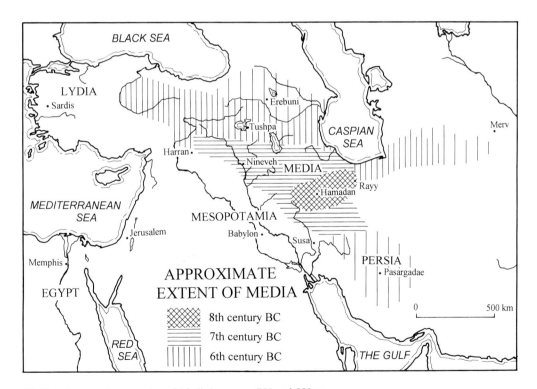

23 Map showing the expansion of Media between c.750 and 550 BC.

mists of time. According to the Mesopotamian scribal tradition, the first cities of Mesopotamia had been founded tens of thousands of years earlier. When the Assyrians first encountered the Medes in the ninth century BC, compared with the peoples of Mesopotamia the Medes were recent arrivals in the Near East.

The population of Mesopotamia was mixed at this time but most people spoke a Semitic language. The language of the cuneiform texts was Akkadian with its two principal dialects of Babylonian and Assyrian (by this time the Sumerian language was a dead language only used by scribes); there were large populations of Aramaic speakers as well as Arabs; and within Mesopotamia there were other minorities such as Kassites and Hurrians who spoke other languages.

The situation in the Zagros is less clear. At the end of the Bronze Age in the late second millennium BC there is evidence for large numbers of peoples being displaced throughout the Near East. Amongst these were the Doric Greeks and the Sea Peoples who destroyed the cities of the Mediterranean and were halted at the borders of Egypt. From the south came Aramaean tribes which settled on the fringes of Mesopotamia. In western Iran too there may have been significant population movements. So-called Early Western Grey Ware pottery is found in the Iron I period in the north and central Zagros (Levine 1987): this ware is not related to earlier Bronze Age pottery of the Zagros, but has been associated with the 'Eastern Grey Ware' of Bronze Age sites to the east of the Caspian Sea. It has long been assumed that the introduction of this pottery was the result of invasions from the northeast and that these invaders were Indo-Iranians, who were the ancestors of the Medes and Persians (e.g. Young 1967).

More recently this identification has been doubted, particularly because the Assyrian records suggest that there were a great variety of different peoples in the Zagros, not all of which were Indo-Iranian and because the excavations at Hasanlu suggest that the art and beliefs of the inhabitants were connected with a Hurrian rather than with an Iranian tradition (Young 1985).

In the following Iron II period, conventionally dated from c.1000–800 BC, there is little evidence from Media. In the northern Zagros at sites such as Hasanlu the Early Western Grey Ware developed into the Late Western Grey Ware. To the south of the Great Khurasan Road is found 'Genre Luristan' painted ware but in the area between there are no certain archaeological remains (Levine 1987). However, this is probably a reflection of our ignorance and should not be interpreted as evidence of lack of settlement in this area.

This absence of evidence is particularly unfortunate as it was during this period that the expanding power of Assyria came into contact with the peoples of the central and northern Zagros (see Luckenbill 1926–7, still the most convenient source for the inscriptions of the later Assyrian kings). In the reigns of Ashurnasirpal II (883–859 BC) and especially his son Shalmaneser III (858–824 BC) the annals of the military campaigns of the Assyrians record victories over regions such as Zamua, Namri, Halman, Mannaea, Gilzanu, Ellipi, Missi, Parsua, and Media. The first mention of the Medes was in 835 BC, the twenty-fourth year of Shalmaneser III. After a successful campaign against Namri, Shalmaneser received the gifts of twenty-seven kings of Parsua and continued his march through the land of the Medes. Since the position of Namri is disputed, some scholars placing it west of Halman along the Diyala river while others locate it to the east of Halman in the Mahi Dasht plain (Levine 1974; Reade 1978), this text leaves the location of the Medes uncertain. In subsequent years the Assyrians frequently attacked the Medes. In the Eponym Chronicle eleven campaigns directed against the Medes were recorded between 821 and 737 BC (Brown 1990b). In the 821 BC campaign the Assyrians defeated a Median ruler called Hanisiruka and destroyed his royal city Sagbitu together with 1200 nearby settlements. Even allowing for the normal exaggeration of the Assyrian royal annals one might expect archaeologists to have found some trace of such settlements.

Assyrian foreign policy was given a new direction by Tiglath-pileser III (744–727 BC). In 737 he annexed the city of Zakruti 'of the mighty Medes' and received tribute from the chiefs of the Medes as far as Mount Bikni, identified by some with Mount Demavend in the Elburz mountains, but thought by others to be a peak in the Zagros (Levine 1974).

Much of the military activity of the reign of Sargon II (721–705 BC) was concerned with the mountainous area to the north and east of Assyria and five of his campaigns took place in the Zagros. The most detailed account is that of 716 BC inscribed on the stele found at Najafehabad in the Assadabad valley (Levine 1972). Much of this campaign seems to have been through Media. Sargon captured Harhar which lay on the western border of Media and renamed it Kar-Sharrukin. He then crossed a river and entered the city of Zakruti, previously annexed by Tiglath-pileser. Here he received the tribute of Daiku, ruler of the city of Shaparda. This name may be compared with that of Deioces, said to have been king of Media by Herodotus. According to Herodotus Deioces united the Medes who before his reign were 'scattered in villages' and founded a central capital at Ecbatana, modern Hamadan. For a while Deioces was identified with a certain Daiukku, a governor of Mannaea, but this identification was rejected by Peyton Helm in his study of Herodotus' Median history, principally because Daiukku was a ruler of Mannaea not Media and was deported to Syria by Sargon II in 715 BC where he died (Helm 1981).

Medes were deported by Tiglath-pileser and Sargon in great numbers (Oded 1979) and deportees from Samaria and north Syria were settled in Media (II Kings XVII.6; Luckenbill 1926–7: II, §183). Occasionally Assyrian texts mention Medes in the service of the army or the court (Harper 1893: nos 174 and 208; Kinnier Wilson 1972: no. 13). On the walls of Sargon's Palace in Dur-Sharrukin (Khorsabad) various peoples are shown bringing gifts to the Assyrian king. Some of these seem to have come from the Zagros mountains (e.g. Albenda 1986: pls 27–34). They carry model cities and bring horses, as the acquisition of horses for the Assyrian army was one of the main aims of Sargon's campaigns against the Medes and other peoples (Figs 24–5). The Zagros-dwellers wear short-sleeved kneelength tunics with belts. Over this they wear animal skins, either sheep skins or leopard skins. They are bare-headed or have hairbands. Their hair is curled sometimes with ringlets, and they sport a variety of beards. They are either barefooted or have high laced-up boots. There are variations in the hairstyles, in the boots and in the clothes which may indicate that these were different peoples but it is impossible now to distinguish Medes, Parsuans, Mannaeans, Ellipians, etc. However, it is likely that some of them were Medes (Wäfler 1975). The Medes (and several other peoples) carved at Bisitun and Persepolis wear a similar tunic but the headgear, cloak, and footwear are different: this is not

24 Drawing of Sargon relief showing Zagros-dwellers bringing horses to Sargon II of Assyria.

25 Drawing of Sargon relief showing Zagros-dwellers wearing skin cloaks.

surprising since the Achaemenid reliefs were carved more than two centuries later, during which period the Medes had gained and lost control of a vast empire (Roaf 1974; Calmeyer 1990). The reliefs also show military campaigns in the Zagros with cities being attacked by the Assyrians. Unfortunately none of the labelled cities on the Assyrian reliefs can be definitely identified as Median but some of them such as Harhar (Fig. 26) and Kishesim were either within Media or on its borders (Gunter 1982; Albenda 1986).

After Sargon the relationship between Assyria and Media changed and only occasionally was military confrontation recorded. The Medes are hardly mentioned in the annals of Sennacherib (704–681 BC). Median chiefs brought horses and lapis lazuli as tribute to his son, Esarhaddon (680–669 BC), in Nineveh. One of these chiefs was Ramataya of Urakazabarna and a copy of the loyalty oath that he swore in 672 to ensure the peaceful succession of Ashurbanipal to the throne of Assyria was found smashed in the Nabu Temple at Kalhu (Parpola and Watanabe 1988).

Esarhaddon's concern for his eastern border is illustrated by the omen texts which record questions put to the sun god (Starr 1990). These show that a threat was posed on the eastern frontier not only by the Medes but also by the Mannaeans and the Ellipians, as well as two other groups, the Gimirrai or Cimmerians and the Ishkuza or Scythians. Several of the omen texts of Esarhaddon are about a certain Kashtaritu, city-ruler of Kar-Kashi, who was making trouble for Assyria. This Kashtaritu has, by a most extraordinary piece of tortuous logic, been associated with another of Herodotus' Median kings, Phraortes, the son of Deioces. The name Phraortes is identified not unreasonably with the Iranian name Fravartish. Now in the Bisitun inscription one of the kings who rebelled against Darius was Fravartish, a Mede, who claimed to be Khshathrita

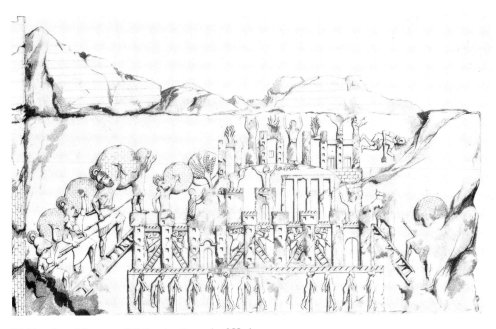

26 Drawing of Sargon relief showing the sack of Harhar.

of the race of Cyaxares. Noting the similarity of Khshathrita with Kashtaritu it was suggested that Kashtaritu was identical with Herodotus' Phraortes (Olmstead 1948: 29). This now seems rather far-fetched. The latest mention of the Medes in the Assyrian texts dates to c.658 BC when Ashurbanipal captured Birishatri, a chief of the Medes and took him to Nineveh (Luckenbill 1926–7: II, §854; Grayson 1980).

According to the Mesopotamian texts from the ninth to the seventh century BC the Medes occupied extensive territories in central western Iran. They were considered as one among many peoples of the Zagros and posed no greater threat to Assyria than Mannaea or Ellipi and probably less threat than Elam or Urartu. The Medes were not united but had numerous rulers. After the first encounter under Shalmaneser III, who mentioned twenty-seven kings of the Medes, the Assyrians called the leaders of the Medes 'city rulers' (*bel alani*). On the other hand Ellipi, Mannaea, and even the Scythians had kings.

But towards the end of the seventh century BC the Medes, allied with the Babylonians, overthrew Assyria. According to a Babylonian chronicle in 615 BC the Medes attacked Arrapha and in 614 captured Tarbisu and Ashur (Grayson 1975). Then two years later the Medes, led by Cyaxares and the Babylonians, led by Nabopolassar, besieged and destroyed Nineveh. The extensive Assyrian empire was divided between the victors. The Babylonians got the southern part and the northern part probably fell to the Medes. Excavations in Assyria have not yet given conclusive proof that the Medes governed rather than just raided the region (Curtis 1989b: 52–4).

In 585 BC according to Herodotus (I.72) Cyaxares made a peace agreement with the Lydians which set the Halys river as the border between their two countries. From this date on the Medes ruled a vast empire stretching from central Turkey to some unidentified region in northeastern Iran or beyond (Fig. 23). Yet almost nothing is known of this period. The contemporary sources are almost entirely silent about the Medes. The cuneiform sources barely mention them, though under the name of Umman-manda their presence may be recorded in the vicinity of Harran at the beginning of the reign of Nabonidus (555–539 BC). The only Medes recorded in the Babylonian texts of this period are Umakishtar (Cyaxares), Ishtumegu (Astyages), and a certain Kurbannu (a name which could also be read Shadbannu or Madbannu) who received rations in Babylon in 591 (Weidner 1939: 930). Even including the names of Medes mentioned in Greek sources referring to the period of the Median empire, such as Harpagos/Arbaces, Mazares, Artembares, and Mitradates, the names of fewer than ten Medes have been preserved for the period of the Median empire. According to the Nabonidus Chronicle in 550 BC Ishtumegu (Astyages, the son of Cyaxares) marched against Cyrus, the ruler of Anshan/Persia (Grayson 1985: 106). The Median army rebelled and Astyages was handed over to Cyrus who marched to the land of Agamtanu (Ecbatana, Hamadan). This was the first major victory of Cyrus and within a dozen years he had conquered the whole of western Asia.

The Evidence from Media: Architecture

Having examined the evidence from Mesopotamia about Media, I will turn to the surviving evidence from Media itself. Hamadan, said in later sources to have been the Median capital, has only been the subject of limited or unauthorised investigations (Col. Pl. XVIII), and no certainly pre-Achaemenid levels have been excavated (Chevalier 1989; Calmeyer 1972). However, traces of mud-brick walls made out of large rectangular mud-bricks are visible where the modern road cuts through the ancient tell (Col. Pl. XIX). These may well be Median as the bricks are rectangular rather than the square bricks normally used in the Achaemenid period.

Two other sites not far from Hamadan have been excavated. These are Tepe Nush-i Jan and Godin Tepe. The pottery from these sites includes Iron III wares which have been dated to the seventh and sixth centuries BC. There are a number of contemporary sites a bit further afield, such as Baba Jan and Surkh Dum in Luristan and Ziwiye and Zendan-i Suleiman in Kurdistan, but despite some similarities in ceramics these sites lie outside the Median heartland: they almost certainly fell under Median control only in the early sixth century. Baba Jan is particularly interesting in this connection since the earlier Level III building was destroyed by fire and the new occupants in Level II used micaceous buff wares of the kind found at Nush-i Jan and Godin. This can easily be interpreted as the result of the expanding territorial control of the Medes.

The site of Nush-i Jan is a religious sanctuary built on the top of a small hill some 70 km southeast of Hamadan (Stronach 1968; Roaf and Stronach 1973; Stronach and Roaf 1978; Curtis 1984). It is a small site with four or five small mud-brick buildings on it (Fig. 27). The earliest was the Central Temple, built on the highest point of the natural shale outcrop. It has an unusual stepped lozenge plan and even more unusually it was carefully filled up with shale and surrounded and capped with mud-brick. For this reason the architecture was very well preserved. Inside the sanctuary was an altar made of mud-brick on which fires had been burnt. The walls of the sanctuary were decorated with elaborate stepped niches with hanging dentils (Pl. 50). The roofs of the antechamber and the spiral ramp in the southwest of the temple were intact when excavated and were constructed using long curved moulded mud-brick struts. This technique is found in the other buildings at Tepe Nush-i Jan and later in Persepolis, Dahan-i Ghulaman, Kuh-i Khwaja, and Shahr-i Qumis in Iran and at Tell Jemmeh in Palestine.

Tepe Nush-i Jan

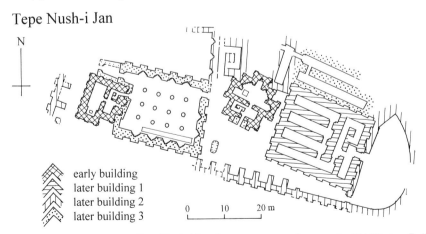

early building
later building 1
later building 2
later building 3

27 Plan of main Median buildings at Tepe Nush-i Jan; from west to east these are the Old Western Building, the Columned Hall, the Central Temple and the Fort.

The next building to be constructed at Tepe Nush-i Jan was a second temple at the western end of the hill (called the Old Western Building). This was built on a mud-brick platform. Traces of an altar were found in the main room which had walls with niches and ventilation holes (Pl. 51). Although superficially these two temples have different plans, functionally they operated in the same way with antechamber, spiral ramp and double height sanctuary with an altar to the left of the doorway.

A third building, called by the excavators the Fort, was constructed to the east of the Central Temple. This had buttressed and recessed façades with arrowslots. Like the temples it had a spiral ramp. Most of the ground floor was taken up with four long narrow magazines lit by small windows close to the ceilings which were again constructed using mud-brick struts. Lower down the walls were pierced by air vents (Pl. 52). Similar vents were found in both the temples and such vents have been also found in Mesopotamia in the fortifications at Ashur and in Building F at Dur-Katlimmu on the Habur River (Andrae 1913: fig. 193; Kühne 1987–8: figs 9 and 11).

Along the southern and western sides of the site rows of arches were found attached to a perimeter wall (Pls 53–4). Because these areas had been filled with mud-brick some of the arches, made out of mud-brick struts, were still preserved. These deep arcades have not been identified on other contemporary sites but constructions with similar groundplans have been excavated in Mesopotamia at Dur-Sharrukin in the Nabu Temple and in the temple area in the Palace (Loud 1936) and at Ur in the Palace of Ennigaldi-Sin (Bel-shalti-Nannar) (Woolley and Mallowan 1962). The original entrance to the Central Temple may have had a similar deep open vaulted chamber. Effectively these arches are the earliest known examples of the vaulted chamber open on one side called an *aivan* or *eyvan* which much later came to dominate Iranian architecture (Keall 1974).

Godin Tepe

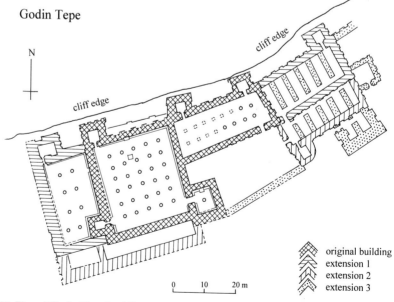

28 Plan of Godin Tepe level II.

A later addition to the site was the Columned Hall, which was built against the western temple, blocking off the original entrance (Fig. 27). This may have replaced an earlier hall built slightly to the north. The columned hall had four rows of three columns. Columned halls are known from an earlier date at Hasanlu in northwest Iran and it is likely that they formed an integral part of the local architectural traditions of Media. In Mesopotamia too, columns were known from an early date and were frequently used in Assyria, but they were placed on façades rather than in halls. The Columned Hall at Tepe Nush-i Jan, like the Central Temple and the earlier northern hall, had decorated niches with stepped sides recalling the elaborate niches on Mesopotamian temples but here with hanging dentils.

The Median building at Godin Tepe was built near the edge of an earlier tell (Young 1969; Young and Levine 1974). Like Nush-i Jan it had a complex sequence of construction and was in use for a long period. But unlike Nush-i Jan, which was primarily a religious sanctuary, Godin appears to have been a more secular settlement consisting of columned halls, storage magazines, and fortified towers (Fig. 28). Most of the column bases were denuded but one example was found with a mud-brick surround similar to those from Nush-i Jan. The outer walls had buttressed and recessed façades with arrowslots. It is easy to see the similarity between these walls and those of the fortresses depicted in the Assyrian reliefs (Gunter 1982).

Thus, although within the Near Eastern tradition of mud-brick architecture, these two sites show an original distinctive architectural style with peculiarities of technique and design not common in Mesopotamia. As one might expect the similarities with Mesopotamia are closest in military architecture, but the Medes did not apparently attempt to emulate the imposing massive architecture of Mesopotamia.

Two further sites on the edge of Mesopotamia may have been built for the Medes. Tell Gubba in Iraq and Tille Höyük in Turkey were both built on earlier settlements, that of Gubba abandoned almost 2000 years earlier. Here a small fort was built using rectangular bricks, which closely parallels in design and construction the Fort at Nush-i Jan (Fujii 1981) (Fig. 29). The building at Tille Höyük beside the Euphrates was also built on top of an earlier tell (French 1986).

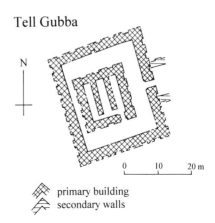

Tell Gubba

N

0   10   20 m

⬧ primary building
⬧ secondary walls

29 Plan of Fort at Tell Gubba.

Tille Höyük

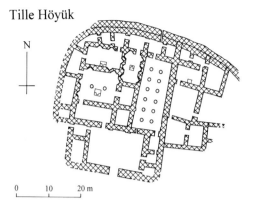

N

0   10   20 m

30 Plan of building at Tille Höyük.

This complex was originally about 60 m in diameter with columned halls and stepped niches like those at Nush-i Jan (Fig. 30). The date of the building is uncertain: it follows one that has Assyrian parallels and it may well have been built in the brief period of Median supremacy after the fall of Assyria and before the rise of Persia.

Conclusion

As these excavations have shown, the Medes created a distinctive architectural style. Median art, however, is a matter of conjecture and is likely to remain so until the royal palaces and tombs are excavated. The Medes were poised to take over the whole of the Near East (Fig. 23). If Astyages had not marched against Cyrus and his army had not mutinied, the Medes rather than the Persians might have conquered southern Mesopotamia. In the event, however, Cyrus, the ruler of the small kingdom of Persia, acquired the extensive Median territories and became known as King of the Medes (Graf 1984). Unable to govern without their help, Cyrus recruited Medes into his service and in his government Medes and Persians played an equal role. With the accession of Darius I, in 521 BC, the role of the Medes was reduced and the Persians were promoted. Despite their pivotal role in the transfer of power from Ancient Mesopotamia to Iran, the Medes are still the least known of the major powers of the Ancient Near East and are likely to remain enigmatic until their archives are discovered.

Note

1 The issues considered here will be discussed in the publication of the architecture and stratigraphy of Tepe Nush-i Jan being prepared by David Stronach and myself. I am grateful to David Stronach, John Curtis, Stephanie Dalley and Nicholas Postgate for advice and information.

There is an extensive secondary literature about the question of Media. Recent discussions include Brown 1986, 1988, 1990a; Dandamaev and Lukonin 1989; Diakonoff 1985; Levine 1987; Muscarella 1987; Sancisi-Weerdenburg 1988; Stronach 1986; Yamauchi 1990; Young 1988; Zawadski 1988.

Bibliography

Albenda, P. 1986. *The Palace of Sargon King of Assyria*, Éditions Recherche sur les Civilisations, Synthèse no. 22, Paris.

Alizadeh, A., 1985. 'A tomb of the Neo-Elamite period at Arjān, near Behbahan', *Archaeologische Mitteilungen aus Iran* 18: 49–73.

Amiet, P., 1966. *Elam*, Auvers-sur-Oise.

Amiet, P., 1972. *Glyptique susienne*, Mémoires de la Délégation Archéologique en Iran 43, Paris.

Amiet, P., 1976a. *Les antiquités du Luristan* (Collection David-Weill), Paris.

Amiet, P., 1976b. 'Disjecta membra aelamica : le décor architectural en briques émaillées à Suse', *Arts Asiatiques* 32: 13–28.

Amiet, P., 1977. *L'art antique du Proche-Orient*, Paris.

Amiet, P., 1986. *L'Âge des Échanges Inter-Iraniens 3500–1700 avant J.-C.*, Notes et Documents des Musées de France 11, Paris.

Amiet, P., 1988. *Suse: 6000 ans d'histoire*, Paris.

Amiet, P., 1990. 'Marlik et Tchoga Zanbil', *Revue d'Assyriologie* 84: 44–7.

Andrae, W. 1913. *Die Festungswerke von Assur*, Wissenschaftliche Veröffentlichungen der Deutschen Orient-Gesellschaft 23, Leipzig.

Andrae, W., 1935. *Die jüngeren Ischtar-Tempel in Assur*, Wissenschaftliche Veröffentlichungen der Deutschen Orient-Gesellschaft 58, Leipzig.

Andrae, W., 1943. *Ausgrabungen in Sendschirli V: Die Kleinfunde*, Berlin.

Andrae, W., 1977. *Das wiedererstandene Assur*, second edition revised and enlarged by B. Hrouda, Munich.

Baker, H.S., 1966. *Furniture in the Ancient World*, London.

Baqir, T., 1944. 'Excavations at 'Aqar Qūf, 1942–1943', *Iraq Supplement*.

Baqir, T., 1945. 'Iraq Government excavations at 'Aqar Qūf: second interim report 1943–1944', *Iraq Supplement*.

Barag, D., 1985. *Catalogue of Western Asiatic Glass in the British Museum* I, London.

Barnett, R.D., 1975. *Catalogue of the Nimrud Ivories*, second edition revised and enlarged, London.

Basmachi, F., 1976. *Treasures of the Iraq Museum*, Baghdad.

Bittel, K., 1976. *Die Hethiter*, Munich.

Boehmer, R.M., 1981. 'Glyptik der späten Kassiten-Zeit aus dem nordöstlichen Babylonien', *Baghdader Mitteilungen* 12: 71–81.

Boehmer, R.M., 1989. Review of *Archaeologische Mitteilungen aus Iran* 18 (1985) in *Zeitschrift für Assyriologie* 79: 142–5.

Börker-Klähn, J., 1982. *Altvorderasiatische Bildstelen und vergleichbare Felsreliefs*, Baghdader Forschungen 4, Mainz am Rhein.

Botta, P.E., 1849–50. *Monument de Ninive*, 5 vols, Paris.

Braun-Holzinger, E.A., 1981. 'Terrakotte eines knieenden Mannes aus Isin', in Hrouda 1981: 62–5.

Brown, S.C., 1986. 'Media and secondary state

formation in the Neo-Assyrian Zagros: an anthropological approach to an Assyriological problem', *Journal of Cuneiform Studies:* 38: 107–19.

Brown, S.C., 1988. 'The Mêdikos Logos of Herodotus and the evolution of the Median state', in Kuhrt, A., and Sancisi-Weerdenburg, H. (eds), *Achaemenid History III: Method and Theory*, Leiden: 71–86.

Brown, S.C., 1990a. 'Media in the Achaemenid period: the Late Iron Age in Central West Iran', in Sancisi-Weerdenburg, H., and Kuhrt, A. (eds.), *Achaemenid History IV: Centre and Periphery*, Leiden: 63–76.

Brown, S.C., 1990b. 'Medien (Media)', *Reallexikon der Assyriologie* VII/7–8: 619–23.

Calmeyer, P., 1969. *Datierbare Bronzen aus Luristan und Kirmanshah*, Untersuchungen zur Assyriologie und Vorderasiatischen Archäologie 5, Berlin.

Calmeyer, P. 1972. 'Hamadan', *Reallexikon der Assyriologie* IV/1: 64–7.

Calmeyer, P., 1973. *Reliefbronzen in babylonischem Stil*, Bayerische Akademie der Wissenschaften, Philosophisch-Historische Klasse 73, Munich.

Calmeyer, P., 1982. 'Mesopotamien und Iran im II. und I. Jahrtausend', in Nissen, H.-J., and Renger, J. (eds.), *Mesopotamien und seine Nachbarn*, 2 vols, Berlin: 339–348.

Calmeyer, P., 1990. 'Tracht der Meder', *Reallexikon der Assyriologie* VII/7–8: 615–7.

Carter, E., and Stolper, M.W., 1984. *Elam: Surveys of Political History and Archaeology*, Berkeley and Los Angeles.

Chevalier, N., 1989. 'Hamadan 1913: une mission oubliée', *Iranica Antiqua* 24: 245–53.

Collon, D., 1994. 'Obituary of Professor Edith Porada', *The Independent*, 4th April: 24.

Curtis, J.E., 1983. 'Late Assyrian bronze coffins', *Anatolian Studies* 33: 85–95.

Curtis, J.E., 1984. *Nush-i Jan III: The Small Finds*, London.

Curtis, J.E., 1989a. *Ancient Persia*, London.

Curtis, J.E., 1989b. *Excavations at Qasrij Cliff and Khirbet Qasrij*, London.

Curtis, J.E., 1993. 'William Kennett Loftus and his excavations at Susa', *Iranica Antiqua* 28: 1–55.

Curtis, J.E., 1994. 'Obituary of Professor Louis Vanden Berghe', *Iran* 32: v-vi.

Curtis, J.E., and Grayson, A.K., 1982. 'Some inscribed objects from Sherif Khan in the British Museum', *Iraq 44:* 87–94.

Curtis, V.S., 1988. 'Report on a recent visit to Iran', *Iran* 26: 145.

Dandamaev, M.A., and Lukonin, V.G., 1989. *The Cultural and Social Institutions of Ancient Iran*, translated from Russian by P. Kohl, Cambridge.

De Clercq-Fobe, D., 1978. *Épingles votives du Luristan (Iran) à disque et plaque en bronze non-ajouré conservées aux Musées Royaux d'Art et d'Histoire de Bruxelles*, Tehran.

De Meyer, L., and Gasche, H. (eds), 1991. *Mesopotamie et Elam: Actes de la XXXVIème Rencontre Assyriologique Internationale, Gand, 10–14 juillet 1989*, Mesopotamian History and Environment, Occasional Publications 1, Gent.

de Miroschedji, P., 1981. 'Le dieu élamite au serpent et aux eaux jaillissantes', *Iranica Antiqua* 16: 1–25.

Diakonoff, I.M., 1985. 'Media', *Cambridge History of Iran* II, Cambridge: 36–148.

Dyson, R.H., Jr., 1957. 'A Gift of Nimrud Sculptures', *Bulletin of the Brooklyn Museum* 18, fascicule 3: 1–12.

Dyson, R.H., Jr., and Muscarella, O.W., 1989. 'Constructing the chronology and historical implications of Hasanlu IV', *Iran* 27: 1–27.

Dyson, R.H., Jr., and Voigt, M.M., 1989. 'East of Assyria: the highland settlement of Hasanlu', *Expedition* 31, nos 2–3, Philadelphia.

Frankfort, H., 1954. *The Art and Architecture of the Ancient Orient*, Pelican History of Art, Harmondsworth.

French, D.H., 1986. 'Tille', *VIII. Kazi Sonuçlari Toplantisi* I, Ankara: 205–12.

Fujii, H., (ed.), 1981. 'Preliminary report of excavations at Gubba and Songor', *Al–Rāfidān* 2: 3–242 (in Japanese and English).

Ghirshman, R., 1968. *Tchoga Zanbil II: Temenos, temples, palais, tombes*, Mémoires de la Délégation Archéologique en Iran 40, Paris.

Ghirshman, R., and Steve, M.-J., 1966. 'Suse. Campagne de l'hiver 1964–1965. Rapport préliminaire', *Arts Asiatiques* 13: 3–32.

Graf, D.F., 1984. 'Medism: the origin and significance of the term', *Journal of Hellenic Studies* 104: 15–30.

Grayson, A.K., 1975. *Assyrian and Babylonian Chronicles*, Texts from Cuneiform Sources 5, Locust Valley, New York.

Grayson, A.K., 1980. 'The chronology of the reign of Ashurbanipal', *Zeitschrift für Assyriologie* 70: 227–45.

Grayson, A.K., 1991. 'Assyria: 744–635 B.C.', chapters 22–24, *Cambridge Ancient History* III/2 (second edition), Cambridge : 71–161.

Gunter, A. 1982. 'Representations of Urartian and western Iranian fortress architecture in the Assyrian reliefs', *Iran* 20: 103–12.

Haller, A., 1954. *Die Gräber und Grüfte von Assur*, Wissenschaftliche Veröffentlichung der Deutschen Orient-Geschschaft 65, Berlin.

Harper, P.O., Aruz, J., and Tallon, F. (eds), 1992. *The Royal City of Susa: Ancient Near Eastern*

Treasures in the Louvre, The Metropolitan Museum of Art, New York.

Harper, R.F. 1893. *Assyrian and Babylonian Letters belonging to the Kouyunjik Collection of the British Museum*, Part II, London.

Helm, P.R., 1981. 'Herodotus' *Mêdikos Logos* and Median history', *Iran* 19: 85–90.

Hogarth, D.G., 1914. *Carchemish I: Introductory*, London.

Howes Smith, P.H.G., 1986. 'A study of 9th-7th century metal bowls from Western Asia', *Iranica Antiqua* 21: 1–88.

Hrouda, B., 1965. *Die Kulturgeschichte des Assyrischen Flachbildes*, Saarbrücker Beiträge zur Altertumskunde 2, Bonn.

Hrouda, B., 1981. *Isin-Išān Bahrīyāt II: die Ergebnisse der Ausgrabungen 1975–1978*, Munich.

Hrouda, B., 1991. *Der Alte Orient: Geschichte und Kultur des alten Vorderasien*, Munich.

Hrouda, B., 1992. *Isin-Išān Bahrīyāt IV: die Ergebnisse der Ausgrabungen 1986–1989*, Munich.

Keall, E.J., 1974. 'Some thoughts on the early *eyvan*', in Kouymjian, D.K. (ed.), *Near Eastern Numismatics, Iconography, Epigraphy and History: Studies in Honor of George C. Miles*, Beirut: 123–30.

Kepinski, C., and Lecomte, O., 1985. 'Haradum, une forteresse sur l'Euphrate', *Archéologia* 205: 46–55.

Kinnier Wilson, J.V., 1972. *The Nimrud Wine Lists*, Cuneiform Texts from Nimrud I, London.

Kramer, S.N., Baqir, T., and Levy, S.J., 1948. 'Fragments of a diorite statue of Kurigalzu in the Iraq Museum', *Sumer* 4: 1–38.

Kühne, H., 1987–8. 'Report on the excavation at Tall Šēh Hamad/Dūr-Katlimmu 1988', *Annales Archéologiques Arabes Syriennes* 37–8: 142–57.

Kurochkin, G.N., 1990. *'A gold vessel from Marlik'*, *Sovetskaya Arkheologiya*, fascicule 2: 41–50.

Labat, R., 1975. 'Elam and Western Persia, *c*.1200–1000 BC', *Cambridge Ancient History* II/2 (third edition), Cambridge: 482–506.

Le Strange, G., 1905. *The Lands of the Eastern Caliphate*, Cambridge.

Levine, L.D., 1972. *Two Neo–Assyrian Stelae from Iran*, Royal Ontario Museum Art and Archaeology Occasional Paper 23, Toronto.

Levine, L.D., 1974. 'Geographical studies in the Neo-Assyrian Zagros – II. The north-eastern Zagros and the Great Khorasan Road', *Iran* 12: 99–124.

Levine, L.D., 1987. 'The Iron Age', in Hole, F. (ed.), *The Archaeology of Western Iran: Settlement and Society from Prehistory to the Islamic Conquest*, Washington: 229–50.

Lianfranchi, G.B., and Parpola, S., 1990. *The Correspondence of Sargon II, Part II*, State Archives of Assyria 5, Helsinki.

Loftus, W.K., 1857. *Travels and Researches in Chaldaea and Susiana*, London.

Loud, G. 1936. *Khorsabad I: Excavations in the Palace and at a City Gate*, Oriental Institute Publications 38, Chicago.

Luckenbill, D.D., 1926–7. *Ancient Records of Assyria and Babylonia*, 2 vols, Chicago.

Lukonin, V.G., 1986. *Kunst des alten Iran*, translated from Russian by S. Grebe, Leipzig.

Madhloom, T.A., 1970. *The Chronology of Neo-Assyrian Art*, London.

Majidzadeh, Y., 1992. 'The Arjan bowl', *Iran* 30: 131–44.

Mallowan, M.E.L., 1966. *Nimrud and its Remains*, 2 vols, London.

Marcus, M.I., 1988. *The Seals and Sealings from Hasanlu IVB, Iran*, Ph.D. Dissertation, University of Pennsylvania, University Microfilms, Ann Arbor.

Marcus, M.I., 1990. 'Centre, *province* and periphery: a new paradigm from Iron-Age Iran', *Art History* 13: 129–50.

Marcus, M.I., 1991. 'The mosaic glass vessels from Hasanlu, Iran: a study in large-scale stylistic trait distribution', *The Art Bulletin* 73: 537–60.

Markoe, G., 1985. 'An Assyrian-style bucket from Chamzhi Mumah, Luristan', *Iranica Antiqua* 20: 43–55.

Matthews, D.M., 1990. *Principles of Composition in Near Eastern Glyptic of the Later Second Millennium BC*, Orbis Biblicus et Orientalis, Series Archaeologica 8, Freiburg and Göttingen.

Matthews, D.M., 1992. *The Kassite Glyptic of Nippur*, Orbis Biblicus et Orientalis 116, Freiburg and Göttingen.

Medvedskaya, I., 1988. 'Who destroyed Hasanlu IV?', *Iran* 26: 1–15.

Medvedskaya, I., 1991. 'Once more on the destruction of Hasanlu IV: problems of dating', *Iranica Antiqua* 26: 149–61.

Moorey, P.R.S., 1971. *Catalogue of the Ancient Persian Bronzes in the Ashmolean Museum*, Oxford.

Moorey, P.R.S., 1974. *Ancient Bronzes from Luristan*, British Museum, London.

Moorey, P.R.S., 1993. Review of Dyson and Voigt 1989 in *Journal of Near Eastern Studies* 52: 319–20.

Mousavi, A., 1994. 'Une brique à décor polychrome de l'Iran occidental (VIIIe-VIIe s. av.J.-C.)', *Studia Iranica* 23: 7–18.

Muscarella, O.W., 1987. 'Median art and Medizing scholarship', *Journal of Near Eastern Studies* 46: 109–27.

Muscarella, O.W., 1988a. *Bronze and Iron. Ancient Near Eastern Artifacts in the Metropolitan Museum of Art*, New York.

Muscarella, O.W., 1988b. 'The background to the Luristan bronzes', in Curtis, J.E. (ed.), *Bronzeworking Centres of Western Asia c.1000–539 BC*, London: 33–44.

Mustafa, M.A., 1947. 'Kassite figurines: a new group discovered near 'Aqar Qûf', *Sumer* 3: 19–22.

Negahban, E.O., 1964. *A Preliminary Report on Marlik*, Tehran.

Negahban, E.O., 1968. 'Marlik: a royal necropolis of the second millennium', *Archaeologia Viva* I: 59–62, 67–79.

Negahban, E.O., 1977. 'The seals of Marlik Tepe', *Journal of Near Eastern Studies* 36: 81–102.

Negahban, E.O., 1983. *Metal Vessels from Marlik*, Prähistorische Bronzefunde II/3, Munich.

Negahban, E.O., 1990. 'Silver vessel of Marlik with gold spout and impressed gold designs', *Acta Iranica* 30 (Papers in honor of Professor Ehsan Yarshater): 144–51.

Negahban, E.O., 1991. *Excavations at Haft Tepe, Iran*, University Museum Monograph 70, Philadelphia.

Oates, D., 1965. 'The excavations at Tell al Rimah, 1964', *Iraq* 27: 62–80.

Oates, D., 1966. 'The excavations at Tell al Rimah, 1965', *Iraq* 28: 122–39.

Oded, B., 1979. *Mass Deportations and Deportees in the Neo-Assyrian Empire*, Wiesbaden.

Olmstead, A.T., 1948. *History of the Persian Empire*, Chicago.

Oppenheim, A.L., 1949. 'The golden garments of the gods', *Journal of Near Eastern Studies* 8: 172–93.

Page, D.L., 1955. *Sappho and Alcaeus: an Introduction to the Study of Ancient Lesbian Poetry*, Oxford.

Parpola, S., and Watanabe, K., 1988. *Neo-Assyrian Treaties and Loyalty Oaths*, State Archives of Assyria 2, Helsinki.

Parrot, A., 1952. 'Les fouilles de Mari': septième campagne (hiver 1951–1952)', *Syria* 29: 183–203.

Parrot, A., 1961. *Nineveh and Babylon*, London.

Parrot, A., 1969. 'De la Méditerranée à l'Iran: masques énigmatiques', *Ugaritica* 6: 409–18.

Peltenburg, E., 1977. 'A faience from Hala Sultan Tekke and second millennium B.C. Western Asiatic pendants depicting females', in Aström, P., *et al.*, *Hala Sultan Tekke* 3, Studies in Mediterranean Archaeology 45/3, Gothenburg: 177–200.

Porada, E., 1965. *Ancient Iran*, London.

Porada, E., 1979. 'Remarks on Mitannian (Hurrian) and Middle Assyrian glyptic art', *Akkadica* 13: 2–15.

Porada, E., 1992. 'Sidelights on life in the 13th and 12th centuries B.C. in Assyria', in Ward, W.A., and Joukowsky, M.S. (eds.), *The Crisis Years: the 12th century B.C. from Beyond the Danube to the Tigris*, Dubuque, Iowa: 182–7.

Pritchard, J.B., 1954. *The Ancient Near East in Pictures*, Princeton.

Reade, J.E., 1976. 'Elam and Elamites in Assyrian sculpture', *Archaeologische Mitteilungen aus Iran* 9: 97–106.

Reade, J.E., 1977. 'Shikaft-i Gulgul: its date and symbolism', *Iranica Antiqua* 12: 33–44.

Reade, J.E., 1978. 'Kassites and Assyrians in Iran', *Iran* 16: 137–43.

Reade, J.E., 1983. *Assyrian Sculpture*, London.

Roaf, M.D., 1974. 'The subject peoples on the base of the statue of Darius', *Cahiers de la Délégation Archéologique Française en Iran* 4: 73–160.

Roaf, M.D., and Stronach, D.B., 1973. 'Tepe Nūsh-i Jān, 1970: second interim report', *Iran* 11: 129–40.

Sancisi–Weerdenburg, H., 1988. 'Was there ever a Median empire?', in Kuhrt, A., and Sancisi-Weerdenburg H. (eds), *Achaemenid History III: Method and Theory*, Leiden: 197–212.

Sarfaraz, A., 1969. 'Archaeological Service of Iran: the discovery of an Assyrian relief', *Iran* 7: 186.

Sarraf, M.R., 1990. 'The bronze bowl of Kidin-Hutran discovered at Arjan, Behbehan', *Athar* 17: 4–61 (in Persian).

Schaeffer, Cl.F.A., 1933. 'Les fouilles de Minet-el-Beida et de Ras-Shamra: quatrième campagne (printemps 1932)', *Syria* 14: 93–127.

Scheil, V., 1939. 'Textes historiques', *Mémoires de la Mission Archéologique de Perse* 28: 1–35.

Schmidt, E.F., van Loon, M.N., and Curvers, H.H., 1989. *The Holmes Expeditions to Luristan*, Oriental Institute Publications 108, Chicago.

Seidl, U., 1965. 'Zur Umarbeitung zweier Stelenbekrönungen aus Susa und anderer altorientalischer Reliefs', *Berliner Jahrbuch für Vor- und Frühgeschichte* 5: 175–86.

Seidl, Uc., 1986a. *Die elamischen Felsreliefs von Kūrāngūn und Naqš-e Rustam*, Iranische Denkmäler 12, Berlin.

Seidl, U., 1986b. Review of Börker-Klähn 1982, in *Orientalia* 55: 320–7.

Seidl, U., 1989. *Die Babylonischen Kudurru-Reliefs*, Orbis Biblicus et Orientalis 87, Freiburg and Göttingen.

Spycket, A., 1981. *La statuaire du Proche-Orient ancien*, Handbuch der Orientalistik VII/1/2/B2, Leiden and Cologne.

Spycket, A., 1992a. *Les figurines de Suse*, Mémoires de la Délégation Archéologique en Iran 52, Paris.

Spycket, A., 1992b. 'Les figurines de terre cuite 1986, 1988–1989 (9e-11e campagnes), in Hrouda 1992: 56–73.

Starr, I., 1990. *Queries to the Sungod: Divination and Politics in Sargonid Assyria*, State Archives of Assyria 4, Helsinki.

Starr, R.F.S., 1937–9. *Nuzi*, 2 vols, Cambridge, Mass.

Strommenger, E., 1964. 'Grabformen in Babylon', *Baghdader Mitteilungen* 3: 157–73.

Strommenger, E., 1967. *Gefässe aus Uruk von der neubabylonischen Zeit bis zu den Sasaniden*, Berlin.

Stronach, D.B., 1959. 'The development of the fibula in the Near East', *Iraq* 21: 181–206.

Stronach, D.B., 1969. 'Excavations at Tepe Nūsh–i Jān, 1967', *Iran* 7: 1–20.

Stronach, D.B., 1986. 'Archaeology: Median and Achaemenid', *Encyclopaedia Iranica* II/3: 288–96.

Stronach, D.B., and Roaf, M.D., 1978. 'Excavations at Tepe Nush-i Jan. Part 1: a third interim report', *Iran* 16: 1–11.

Thureau-Dangin, F., 1930. 'Un spécimen des peintures assyriennes de Til-Barsip', *Syria* 11: 113–32.

Thureau-Dangin, F., *et al.*, 1931. *Arslan-Tash*, Paris.

Thureau-Dangin, F., and Dunand, M., 1936. *Til-Barsib*, Paris.

Vallat, F., 1984. 'Kidin-Hutran et l'époque néo-élamite', *Akkadica* 37: 1–17.

Vanden Berghe, L., 1967. 'La nécropole de War Kabud', *Archéologia* 18: 48–61.

Vanden Berghe, L., 1968. *Het archeologisch onderzoek naar de Bronscultuur van Luristan. Opgravingen in Pusht-i Kuh. I. Kalwali-War Kabud (1965–1966)*, Brussels.

Vanden Berghe, L., 1970. 'Prospections archéologiques de la région de Badr', *Archéologia* 36: 10–21.

Vanden Berghe, L., 1971. 'La nécropole de Bard-i Bal au Luristan', *Archéologia* 43: 14–23.

Vanden Berghe, L., 1973a. 'La nécropole de Kutal-i Gulgul', *Archéologia* 65: 16–29.

Vanden Berghe, L., 1973b. 'Pusht-i Kūh, Luristan', in 'Survey of excavations in Iran 1971–72', *Iran* 11: 207–9.

Vanden Berghe, L., 1979. 'Les bronzes du Luristan de l'âge du fer III: résultats des fouilles au Pusht-i Kuh', in *Akten des VII. Internationalen Kongresses für Iranische Kunst und Archäologie, München, 7.-10. September 1976, Archäologische Mitteilungen aus Iran, Ergänzungsband* 6, Berlin: 138–50.

Vanden Berghe, L., 1987. 'Les pratiques funéraires à l'âge du Fer III au Pusht-i Kuh, Luristan: les nécropoles 'genre War Kabud'', *Iranica Antiqua* 22: 201–66.

Vanden Berghe, L., and Smekens, E., 1984. *Reliefs rupestres de l'Irān Ancien*, Catalogue of exhibition at Musées Royaux d'Art et d'Histoire, Brussels.

Van Dijk, J., 1986. 'Die dynastischen Heiraten zwischen Kassiten und Elamern: eine verhängnisvolle Politik', *Orientalia* 55: 159–70.

Wäfler, M. 1975. *Nicht-Assyrer neuassyrischer Darstellungen*, Alter Orient und Altes Testament 26, Neukirchen-Vluyn.

Weidner, E.F., 1939. 'Jojachin, König von Juda, in babylonischen Keilschrifttexten', in *Mélanges syriens offerts à Monsieur René Dussaud*, Bibliothèque Archéologique et Historique 30, Paris: 923–35.

Winter, I.J., 1977. 'Perspective on the 'Local Style' of Hasanlu IVB: a study in receptivity', in Levine, L.D., and Young T.C. (eds), *Mountains and Lowlands*, Bibliotheca Mesopotamica 7, Malibu: 371–86.

Woolley, C.L., 1952. *Carchemish III: The Excavations in the Inner Town*, London.

Woolley, C.L., 1965. *Ur Excavations VIII: The Kassite Period and the Period of the Assyrian Kings*, London.

Woolley, C.L., and Mallowan, M.E.L., 1962. *Ur Excavations IX: The Neo-Babylonian and Persian Periods*, London.

Yamauchi, E.M., 1990. *Persia and the Bible*, Grand Rapids, Michigan.

Young, T.C., 1967. 'The Iranian migration into the Zagros', *Iran* 5: 11–34.

Young, T.C., 1969. *Excavations at Godin Tepe: First Progress Report*, Royal Ontario Museum Art and Archaeology Occasional Paper 17, Toronto.

Young, T.C., 1985. 'Early Iron Age Iran revisited: preliminary suggestions for the re-analysis of old constructs', in Huot, J.-L., Yon, M., and Calvet, Y. (eds), *De l'Indus aux Balkans: Recueil à la mémoire de Jean Deshayes*, Paris: 361–78.

Young, T.C., 1988. 'The early history of the Medes and the Persians and the Achaemenid empire to the death of Cambyses', *Cambridge Ancient History* IV (second edition), Cambridge: 1–52.

Young, T.C., and Levine, L.D., 1974. *Excavations of the Godin Project: Second Progress Report*, Royal Ontario Museum Art and Archaeology Occasional Paper 26, Toronto.

Zawadzki, S., 1988. *The Fall of Assyria and Median-Babylonian Relations in the Light of the Nabopolassar Chronicle*, Poznan.

Illustration Acknowledgements

Abbreviation:
BM = Photo by courtesy of the Trustees of the British Museum

Figures
1 BM.
2 BM.
3 BM.
4 BM.
5 From Reade J. E., *Mesopotamia*, London 1991: fig. 1.
6 After Curtis 1989: fig.1.
7 From Alizadeh 1985: figs 2–4.
8 From Curtis 1984: fig. 4/233–4, 236.
9 From Seidl 1989: fig. 22 on p. 60.
10 From Amiet 1972: pl. 35, nos. 2015–2017.
11 From Marcus 1991: fig. 7.
12 From Boehmer 1981: pl. 4, no. 6.
13 From Calmeyer 1973: fig. 132.
14 From Seidl 1986a: fig. 9.
15 From Porada 1965: fig. 60.
16 From Seidl 1986b: fig. on p. 326.
17 From Calmeyer 1982: pl. XXXVI.
18 From Matthews 1992: no. 48.
19 From Calmeyer 1973: fig. 134.
20 From Calmeyer 1973: fig. on p. 45.
21 Map drawn by Michael Roaf.
22 Map drawn by Michael Roaf.
23 Map drawn by Michael Roaf.
24 From Botta 1849–50: II, pl. 126.
25 From Botta 1849–50: II, pl. 136.
26 From Botta 1849–50: I, pl. 55.
27 Plan Michael Roaf.
28 Plan Michael Roaf.
29 Plan Michael Roaf.
30 Plan Michael Roaf.

Black and white plates
1 BM 123061, 123060.
2 From Amiet 1988: fig. 63.
3 Iraq Museum.
4 BM.
5 From Andrae 1935: pl. 48d.
6 BM 124693.
7 From Spycket 1981: pl. 199.
8 Musée du Louvre, Sb 5089–5090. Photo Chuzeville.
9 Musée du Louvre, Sb 3557. Photo El. Le Breton.
10 Musée du Louvre, Sb 2758 Photo Chuzeville.
11 Musée du Louvre, Sb 5889. Photo El. Le Breton.
12 Musée du Louvre, Sb 5638. Photo Chuzeville.
13 Musée du Louvre, Sb 6442. Photo Chuzeville.
14 From Andrae 1935: pl. 34e.
15 Musée du Louvre, Sb 7638, 6611. Photo El. Le Breton.
16 Iraq Museum.
17 Musée du Louvre, Sb 17,755. Photo El. Le Breton.
18 Musée du Louvre, Sb 7797. Photo El. Le Breton.
19 Musée du Louvre, Sb 7476. Photo El. Le Breton.
20 Musée du Louvre, Sb 3588. Photo El. Le Breton.
21 Musée du Louvre, Sb 2899/6592–3. Photo Antiquités Orientales.
22 Musée du Louvre, Sb 6767. Photo Antiquités Orientales.
23 From Negahban 1991: pl. 24/167.
24 From Marcus 1991: fig. 23b.
25 BM 123062.
26 From Schmidt *et al.* 1989: pl. 253, no. XXXV.
27–9 Photographs B. Grunewald.

30 From Schmidt *et al.* 1989: pl. 208c.
31 From Negahban 1983: 39, pl. 12.
32 From Schmidt *et al.* 1989: pl. 255, no. 224.
33 From Negahban 1964: fig. 81.
34 From Negahban 1977: fig. 1.
35 Photo E. Smekens.
36 Photo E. Smekens.
37 Photo E. Smekens.
38 Photo E. Smekens.
39 Photo E. Smekens.
40 Photo Belgian Archaeological Expedition to Luristan.
41 Photo Belgian Archaeological Expedition to Luristan.
42 Photo E. Smekens.
43 Photo E. Smekens.
44 Photo Belgian Archaeological Expedition to Luristan.
45 Photo Belgian Archaeological Expedition to Luristan.
46 Photo E. Smekens.
47 Photo E. Smekens.
48 Photo Belgian Archaeological Expedition to Luristan.
49 Photo Belgian Archaeological Expedition to Luristan.
50 Photo Michael Roaf.
51 Photo Michael Roaf.
52 Photo Michael Roaf.
53 Photo Michael Roaf.
54 Photo Michael Roaf.

Colour Plates
I BM 130905.
II BM 134387.
III BM 134901.
IV From Negahban 1964: pl. XVII.
V Photo John Curtis.
VI Photo John Curtis.
VII BM 135947–8, 135950, 135952.
VIII Photo Stupp.
IX From Parrot 1961: fig. 335.
X BM 113886.
XI Iraq Museum, Photo Stupp.
XII Photo A. Spycket.
XIII From Negahban 1968: pl. XXXII.
XIV–XV From Negahban 1983: pls. on pp. 34–5.
XVI Photo Michael Roaf.
XVII Photo Michael Roaf.
XVIII Photo Michael Roaf.
XIX Photo Michael Roaf.

2 Parts of moulded brick panel of king Shilhak-Inshuskinak in Musée du Louvre.

1 Bronze daggers inscribed with the names of Marduk-nadin-ahhe, king of Babylon, and the eunuch Shamash-killani.

4 Limestone head of a woman from Ur.

3 Painted terracotta head of a man from 'Aqar Quf.

5 Alabaster head of a woman from Ashur.

76

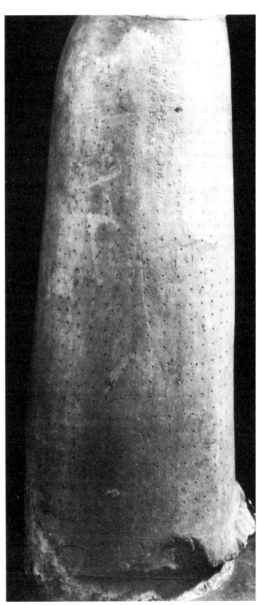

6 Statue from Nineveh inscribed by the king Ashur-bel-kala.

7 Fragment of limestone statue of king Untash-Napirisha from Susa.

8a-b Faience statuette and head from Choga Zanbil.

9 Faience head of a man from Susa.

10 Gold statuette of a worshipper from Susa.

11 Limestone statuette of a woman from Susa.

12 Ivory head of a woman from Susa.

13 Limestone head of a woman with a diadem of snakes, from Susa.

14 Faience statuette of a standing man from Ashur.

15 Terracotta figurines of naked women from Susa.

16 Terracotta disc with figures in relief.

17 Terracotta figurine of a naked woman from Susa.

18 Terracotta figurine of a naked woman from Susa.

19 Terracotta figurine of a dressed woman from Susa.

20 'Frit' mask from Susa.

21 Faience worshipper statuettes from Susa.

22 Female funerary head in painted unbaked clay from Susa.

23 Painted female head in clay from Haft Tepe.

24 Stone bowl of Kadashman-Enlil from Hasanlu.

25 Bronze bowl said to have been found near Kermanshah.

26 Bronze signet-ring from Surkh Dum-i Luri with modern impression, now in Metropolitan Museum of Art, New York.

27-9 Impressions of cylinder seals from Surkh Dum-i Luri, now in Archaeological Museum, Tehran.

30 Fragment of bronze pin-head from Surkh Dum-i Luri.

31 Gold beaker with winged monsters from Marlik.

32 Impression of a cylinder seal said to be from Dilfan province, Luristan.

33 Bronze signet-ring from Marlik.

34 Cylinder seal with modern impression from Marlik.

35 Pear-shaped vessels from War Kabud.

36 Animal-shaped vessel from Djub-i Gauhar.

37 Swords or daggers of Iron Age III date from the Pusht-i Kuh, Luristan.

38 Swords or daggers of Iron Age III date from the Pusht-i Kuh, Luristan.

39 Different types of macehead from Chamzhi-Mumah.

40 Macehead in form of a rosette from War Kabud.

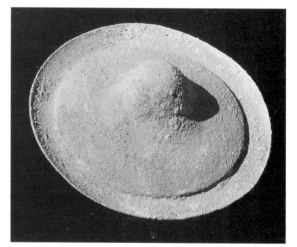

41 (left) Bronze quiver from War Kabud.
42 (above) Bronze shields with central conical boss from Chamzhi-Mumah.

43 Decorated bronze bowl from Chamzhi-Mumah.

44 Bronze pyxis from War Kabud.

45 Bronze situla from War Kabud.

46 Bronze strainer from Chamzhi-Mumah.

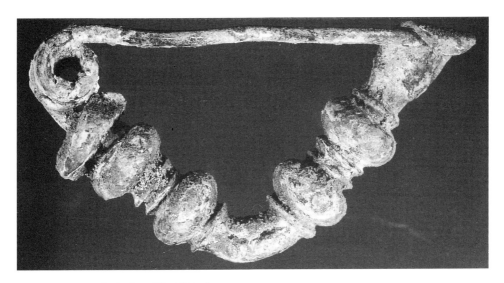

47 Elbow-shaped fibula from War Kabud.

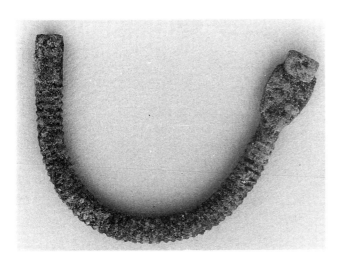

48 Semi-circular fibula from War Kabud.

49 Two types of earrings from War Kabud.

50 The Central Temple at Tepe Nush-i Jan showing the altar and two decorated niches.

51 The Old Western Building at Tepe Nush-i Jan showing a niche and ventilation holes through the wall.

52 One of the rooms in the Fort at Tepe Nush-i Jan showing a high window and a low-level
ventilation hole.

53 The row of arches south of the Central Temple at Tepe Nush-i Jan.

54 A detail of one of the semicircular arches at Tepe Nush-i Jan which was preserved by being encased with mud-bricks. The bricks have not been removed from within the arch.

I *Left* Bronze beaker with lid, probably from Western Iran.

II *Right* Silver beaker probably from Marlik area.

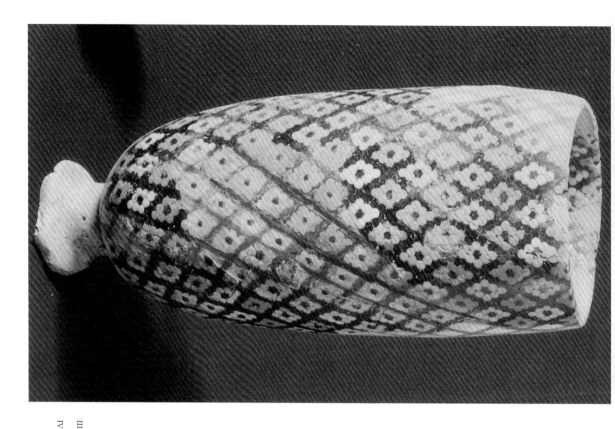

III *Above* Mosaic glass from Tell al-Rimah.

IV *Left* Mosaic glass beaker from Marlik.

v View of Burnt Building II at Hasanlu, partially restored.

VI Distant view of Assyrian rock relief at Tang-i Var, Iran.

VII Selection of pottery from Tepe Nush-i Jan in the British Museum.

VIII *Above* Painted terracotta figure of a man from Isin, Iraq Museum.

IX *Right* Wall painting from palace of king Kurigalzu at 'Aqar Quf.

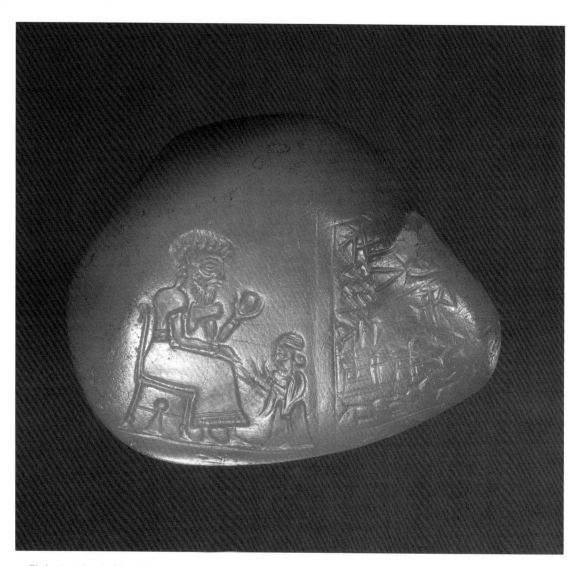

x Chalcedony bead of Bar-Uli, daughter of king Shilhak-Inshushinak.

XI Limestone statuette of a kneeling man from Isin, Iraq Museum.

XII Mrs Tania Ghirshman, Father M.J. Steve and H. Gasche excavating a vaulted tomb with funerary heads at Susa in 1965.

XIII Gold bowl with rams from Marlik.

XIV-XV *Above* Two views of gold beaker with winged bulls from Marlik.

XVI *Opposite top* Dur-Sharrukin (Khorsabad) in northern Mesopotamia.

XVII *Opposite bottom* Tepe Nush-i Jan in Media: the site can be seen in front of the high ridges of the Zagros mountains.

XVIII *Top* View of the ruins of Hamadan, once capital of Media.

XIX A wall at Hamadan, perhaps of Median date.